The Prayer Life
DEVOTIONAL

The Prayer Life
DEVOTIONAL

A Covering For Your (Future) Husband

DR. YVETTE MAUREEN

Copyright © 2020 Dr. Yvette Maureen

All rights reserved. No part of this book may be reproduced, stored, or transmitted by any means—whether auditory, graphic, mechanical, or electronic—without written permission of both publisher and author, except in the case of brief excerpts used in critical articles and reviews. Unauthorized reproduction of any part of this work is illegal and is punishable by law.

Because of the dynamic nature of the Internet, any web addresses or links contained in this book may have changed since publication and may no longer be valid. The views expressed in this work are solely those of the author and do not necessarily reflect the views of the publisher, and the publisher hereby disclaims any responsibility for them.

Guided Prayers For Those:

Preparing their heart for marriage

Trusting God for a godly
marriage and spouse

Seeking to cover a current or
future spouse in prayer

Prioritizing becoming a godly spouse

Ordering their steps in marriage
to honor God's Word

#ThePrayerLifeDevotional
@ThePrayerLife.Devotional

Dear Readers,

The Prayer Life Devotional was created to support women *and* men in your prayer journey as you prepare your heart, your soul, and your spirit to receive God's divine blessings in your relationships.

As the author of *The Fit Life: A Wellness Journal* and as a business scholar, I've written the devotionals as books of guided prayers.

From married couples and dating individuals to those who are single, ready, and frustrated at the same time, we all could use prayer. You know, there's beauty in knowing someone prays for you without you even knowing. That is a deep, pure love we all desire, and with the devotional, it's possible.

The books will guide you daily as you pursue a heart of thanksgiving for a *new* or *renewed* romantic relationship. So, join us on *The Prayer Life Devotional* journey and watch God work *in* and *through* you to give you the desires of your heart.

Blessings,

Dr. Yvette Maureen

CONTENTS

Strength 1

Focus 33

Thanksgiving 65

Humility 101

Grace 131

Wisdom 159

Protection 191

Peace 223

Faith 255

Love 287

Restoration 319

Trust 351

Strength

DAY 1

Dear God,

Empower My Husband to stand firm in your Will, mature and fully assured. Make him a man of strong character and clear convictions that help him to be immovably secure in a shaky world.
In Jesus' name I pray, Amen.

● ● ●

And now, dear brothers and sisters, one final thing. Fix your thoughts on what is true, and honorable, and right, and pure, and lovely, and admirable. Think about things that are excellent and worthy of praise.
Philippians 4:8

DAY 2

Dear God,

Thank You for filling My Husband with the power of the Holy Spirit and strengthening his stance with the teachings in your Word. In Jesus' name I pray, Amen.

* * *

With all these things in mind, dear brothers, and sisters, stand firm and keep a strong grip on the teaching we passed on to you both in person and by letter.
2 Thessalonians 2:15

DAY 3

Dear God,

When My Husband feels worn out or overwhelmed, I pray he will come to You and rest in You. I pray he will take off the yoke of self-sufficiency and put on the yoke of Christ-sufficiency. Help him embrace "I can do all things through Christ who gives me strength." In Jesus' name I pray, Amen.

• • •

Then Jesus said, "Come to me, all of you who are weary and carry heavy burdens, and I will give you rest. Take my yoke upon you. Let me teach you, because I am humble and gentle at heart, and you will find rest for your souls. For my yoke is easy to bear, and the burden I give you is light."
Matthew 11:28-30

DAY 4

Dear God,

When My Husband feels too weak, timid, or inadequate to meet the challenges of life, infuse him with your strength. Assure him that You have given him everything he needs for life and godliness through his knowledge of Jesus. Move him to plug into your power and access your strength.
In Jesus' name I pray, Amen.

• • •

By his divine power, God has given us everything we need for living a godly life. We have received all of this by coming to know him, the one who called us to himself by means of his marvelous glory and excellence.
2 Peter 1:3

DAY 5

Dear God,

Teach My Husband the secret to contentment—whatever we have and wherever we are, we can do all things through Christ who gives us strength. In Jesus' name I pray, Amen.

• • •

I know how to live on almost nothing or with everything. I have learned the secret of living in every situation, whether it is with a full stomach or empty, with plenty or little. For I can do everything through Christ, who gives me strength.
Philippians 4:12-13

DAY 6

Dear God,

Thank You for making My Husband such an encourager that builds others up instead of tearing them down. Continue to propel him forward.
In Jesus' name I pray, Amen.

* * *

Stay away from every kind of evil.
1 Thessalonians 5:22

STRENGTH

DAY 7

Dear God,

Thank You that My Husband is a part of a chosen generation and a royal priesthood according to your Word. He is adorned with a kingly anointing and should never underestimate his strength through You. Remind My Husband that he commands a power to change the course of his destiny. In Jesus' name I pray, Amen.

• • •

> But you are not like that, for you are a chosen people. You are royal priests, a holy nation, God's very own possession. As a result, you can show others the goodness of God, for he called you out of the darkness into his wonderful light.
> 1 Peter 2:9

DAY 8

Dear God,

Strengthen My Husband's courage and confidence in You so that he will not be afraid when trials and difficulties shake his world. Just as the Israelites stood firm to witness your deliverance, empower My Husband to stand firm in his faith to witness your working in his life. Help him not to worry nor fret, but to rest secure in the knowledge of your protection and provision.
In Jesus' name I pray, Amen.

• • •

But Moses told the people, "Don't be afraid. Just stand still and watch the Lord rescue you today. The Egyptians you see today will never be seen again. The Lord himself will fight for you. Just stay calm."
Exodus 14:13-14

DAY 9

Dear God,

Please remind My Husband that You go before him and are always with him; that You will never leave or forsake him. Strengthen My Husband's faith so that he will not be afraid of what the future holds or discouraged when circumstances do not turn out the way he had hoped. Help him to trust in your sovereign plan. In Jesus' name I pray, Amen.

• • •

Do not be afraid or discouraged, for the Lord will personally go ahead of you. He will be with you; he will neither fail you nor abandon you."
Deuteronomy 31:8

DAY 10

Dear God,

Just as You commanded Joshua to be strong and courageous, empower My Husband to be strong and courageous as he does the work You have called him to do. Prompt him to hold on to the mighty promises in your Word.
In Jesus' name I pray, Amen.

• • •

Then the Lord commissioned Joshua son of Nun with these words: "Be strong and courageous, you must bring the people of Israel into the land I swore to give them. I will be with you."
Deuteronomy 31:23

STRENGTH

DAY 11

Dear God,

As My Husband faces his day, help him be strong and courageous to do the work You have called him to do. I pray he will not be afraid or discouraged. Let My Husband know that You are with him to sustain him when he grows weary and to strengthen him when he grows weak. In Jesus' name I pray, Amen.

• • •

Then David continued, "Be strong and courageous, and do the work. Do not be afraid or discouraged, for the Lord God, my God, is with you. He will not fail you or forsake you. He will see to it that all the work related to the Temple of the Lord is finished correctly.
1 Chronicles 28:20

DAY 12

Dear God,

Please give My Husband
physical, emotional, and
spiritual strength today.
In Jesus' name I pray, Amen.

• • •

Wealth and honor come from you alone, for
you rule over everything. Power and might
are in your hand, and at your discretion
people are made great and given strength.
1 Chronicles 29:12

DAY 13

Dear God,

Thank You for strengthening My Husband's heart as he fully commits to You. Empower him to exercise his faith regularly so that You can increase his strength spiritually.
In Jesus' name I pray, Amen.

• • •

The eyes of the Lord search the whole earth to strengthen those whose hearts are fully committed to him. What a fool you have been! From now on you will be at war."
2 Chronicles 16:9

DAY 14

Dear God,

Empower My Husband to pray effectively and strategically according to your perfect will for his life.
In Jesus' name I pray, Amen.

• • •

I tell you, you can pray for anything, and if you believe that you have received it, it will be yours.
Mark 11:24

STRENGTH

DAY 15

Dear God,

When My Husband is discouraged, help him find strength in You just like David did. I pray that My Husband will not depend on people, possessions, or position to lift him up, but that he finds strength, hope, and encouragement in You.
In Jesus' name I pray, Amen.

* * *

Do not be afraid, for I am with you. Do not be discouraged, for I am your God. I will strengthen you and help you. I will hold you up with my victorious right hand.
1 Samuel 30:6

DAY 16

Dear God,

Your Word declares that You will speak to us in dreams and visions, and what You reveal will prosper according to your Word. The dreams that My Husband has are your dreams. Help My Husband to seek You daily for the wisdom and the character to see them come into fruition. Give him supernatural strength and power to live out that dream every day and to complete the mission You have assigned him. I declare that nothing will stop the dreams You have placed in his heart. Thank You for seeing them through to completion. In Jesus' name I pray, Amen.

* * *

And I am certain that God, who began the good work within you, will continue his work until it is finally finished on the day when Christ Jesus returns.
Philippians 1:6

DAY 17

Dear God,

Thank You for being My Husband's strength and shield. No matter what he faces today, prompt My Husband to trust You fully and confidently so that he will not move unless You move.
In Jesus' name I pray, Amen.

• • •

The Lord is my strength and shield. I trust him with all my heart. He helps me, and my heart is filled with joy. I burst out in songs of thanksgiving.
Psalm 28:7

DAY 18

Dear God,

I thank You that You are always working on our behalf even when we cannot see the results. Help My Husband to remain steadfast in prayer today, knowing that in due season he will reap. Bring about your purposes in their correct time. I pray that My Husband waits patiently for You, knowing the answer is on the way. In Jesus' name I pray, Amen.

• • •

For God is the one who provides seed for the farmer and then bread to eat. In the same way, he will provide and increase your resources and then produce a great harvest of generosity in you.
2 Corinthians 9:10

STRENGTH

DAY 19

Dear God,

We come into agreement with the words You have spoken to My Husband. Open his heart to receive a fresh revelation from You today. When My Husband is tired, give him stamina to press forward. Strengthen his body, his mind, and his spirit. In Jesus' name I pray, Amen.

* * *

But those who trust in the Lord will find new strength. They will soar high on wings like eagles. They will run and not grow weary. They will walk and not faint.
Isaiah 40:31

DAY 20

Dear God,

Please give My Husband a well-instructed tongue. Help him to know just the right words to say to someone who is discouraged or depressed. Help his words to give strength to those in need. In Jesus' name I pray, Amen.

• • •

The Sovereign Lord has given me his words of wisdom, so that I know how to comfort the weary.
Isaiah 50:4a

DAY 21

Dear God,

Thank You that My Husband uses his influence to bring your kingdom and to make a difference in this world. Help My Husband to walk boldly in his purpose today and every day, knowing that You have given him authority over the enemy. I pray that nothing will hinder your plans and purposes. Your kingdom will come, and your will shall be done. In Jesus' name I pray, Amen.

• • •

Look, I have given you authority over all the power of the enemy, and you can walk among snakes and scorpions and crush them. Nothing will injure you.
Luke 10:19

DAY 22

Dear God,

We know that the enemy fights us in the area he fears us the most. That is why we take our stand in prayer. Thank You for equipping My Husband with the mind of Christ. May he be bold and courageous to stand firm, to achieve and exceed all his goals, and to accomplish everything You have planned for his life. Your plans will come to pass. In Jesus' name I pray, Amen.

• • •

For God has not given us a spirit of fear and timidity, but of power, love, and self-discipline.
2 Timothy 1:7

STRENGTH

DAY 23

Dear God,

Thank You for hearing and answering our prayers. Help My Husband to listen for your voice. Open his spiritual ears to hear You clearly. Create in him a heart that is receptive to the things of the Spirit and give him prophetic discernment and direction. I pray that My Husband's strength is renewed today as he spends time in your presence.
In Jesus' name I pray, Amen.

* * *

Anyone who belongs to God listens gladly to the words of God. But you do not listen because you do not belong to God.
John 8:47

DAY 24

Dear God,

The primary way You speak to us is through your Word. Because My Husband neglects neither your Word nor your Spirit, his footing is firm, and the power of God is at work in and through him. Thank You for equipping My Husband to destroy the works of the enemy and thank You that he advances your kingdom agenda. In Jesus' name I pray, Amen.

• • •

All Scripture is inspired by God and is useful to teach us what is true and to make us realize what is wrong in our lives. It corrects us when we are wrong and teaches us to do what is right.
2 Timothy 3:16

DAY 25

Dear God,

Give My Husband the strength and stamina to stand firm in his faith through the ups and downs of life. Increase My Husband's faith and make him a man of courage and confidence who does not buckle under pressure—a Man of God who holds his ground. In Jesus' name I pray, Amen.

• • •

Be on guard. Stand firm in the faith.
Be courageous. Be strong.
1 Corinthians 16:13

DAY 26

Dear God,

Fill My Husband with your strength so that he will not waiver in his beliefs but stand firm in his faith. Thank You for anointing him, setting your seal of ownership on him, and putting your Holy Spirit in his heart as a deposit guaranteeing what is to come.
In Jesus' name I pray, Amen.

• • •

It is God who enables us, along with you, to stand firm for Christ. He has commissioned us, and he has identified us as his own by placing the Holy Spirit in our hearts as the first installment that guarantees everything he has promised us.
2 Corinthians 1:21-22

STRENGTH

DAY 27

Dear God,

Thank You for equipping us with life-altering and world-changing power. Give My Husband enormous innovative, creative, and re-creative power with every Word he speaks. I see no impossibilities for My Husband, only chances for You to show your strength on his behalf. Anoint My Husband for this season and time.
In Jesus' name I pray, Amen.

• • •

You won't be able to say, 'Here it is!' or 'It's over there!' For the Kingdom of God is already among you.
Luke 17:21

DAY 28

Dear God,

Strengthen My Husband to be a vessel filled with the power of the Holy Spirit—a strength that can only come from You.
In Jesus' name I pray, Amen.

• • •

We now have this light shining in our hearts, but we ourselves are like fragile clay jars containing this great treasure. This makes it clear that our great power is from God, not from ourselves.
2 Corinthians 4:7

DAY 29

Dear God,

We sit at your feet today and listen for your voice. Thank You that My Husband gains strength from your presence. Thank You that My Husband's perspectives change in your presence.
Take him deeper in You.
In Jesus' name I pray, Amen.

* * *

You will show me the way of life, granting me the joy of your presence and the pleasures of living with you forever
Psalm 16:11

DAY 30

Dear God,

Remind My Husband that his struggle is not against flesh and blood, but against evil forces. Prompt My Husband to put on the full armor of God from head to toe, so that he will have done everything to stand firm when the enemy attacks. Empower My Husband to take his stand and not let the enemy take one inch of conquered ground. In Jesus' name I pray, Amen.

* * *

For we are not fighting against flesh-and-blood enemies, but against evil rulers and authorities of the unseen world, against mighty powers in this dark world, and against evil spirits in the heavenly places. Therefore, put on every piece of God's armor so you will be able to resist the enemy in the time of evil. Then after the battle you will still be standing firm.
Ephesians 6:12–13

STRENGTH

Focus

DAY 31

Dear God,

Guide My Husband's feet today so that he will walk in the light of Christ. Keep him from stumbling about in confusion or uncertainty and light his path so that he can walk secure in You.
In Jesus' name I pray, Amen.

• • •

Jesus spoke to the people once more and said "I am the light of the world. If you follow me, you will not have to walk in darkness, because you will have the light that leads to life.
John 8:12

DAY 32

Dear God,

I pray My Husband's thoughts are steady and unwavering. Help him to trust You wholeheartedly. Replace all doubt and worry with belief and peace.
In Jesus' name I pray, Amen.

• • •

If you need wisdom, ask our generous God, and he will give it to you. He will not rebuke you for asking. But when you ask him, be sure that your faith is in God alone. Do not waver, for a person with divided loyalty is as unsettled as a wave of the sea that is blown and tossed by the wind.
James 1:5-6

FOCUS

DAY 33

Dear God,

Open My Husband's eyes to see your Glory all around. Help him notice your handiwork in the small and the large. Help him to pay attention and not miss your fingerprints throughout the day. In Jesus' name I pray, Amen.

• • •

They were calling out to each other, "Holy, holy, holy is the Lord of Heaven's Armies! The whole earth is filled with his glory!"
Isaiah 6:3

DAY 34

Dear God,

Help My Husband to refuse to listen to men whose ideas of right and wrong change with the seasons. May he eagerly listen to your Word which remains the same yesterday, today, and forever.
In Jesus' name I pray, Amen.

* * *

For a time is coming when people will no longer listen to sound and wholesome teaching. They will follow their own desires and will look for teachers who will tell them whatever their itching ears want to hear. They will reject the truth and chase after myths.
2 Timothy 4:3-4

DAY 35

Dear God,

Prompt My Husband to walk away from foolish talk. May he refuse to listen to conversations that are unworthy of his attention. Keep him focused on the thoughts You desire to enter his mind through what he listens to today.
In Jesus' name I pray, Amen.

* * *

Obscene stories, foolish talk, and coarse jokes—these are not for you. Instead, let there be thankfulness to God.
Ephesians 5:4

DAY 36

Dear God,

Help My Husband to impact the trajectory of his life simply by diligently guarding his heart. Teach him to hide your Word in his heart. Cause your Word to change the way My Husband thinks, the way he speaks, and the way he lives. Help him to seek You with all his heart. In Jesus' name I pray, Amen.

• • •

Guard your heart above all else, for it determines the course of your life.
Proverbs 4:23

FOCUS

DAY 37

Dear God,

Keep My Husband on the right path today. Enoch walked with You and Noah walked with You. May My Husband be known as a man who walks with You. Lead him. Guide him. Show him your way. Father, do not let him run ahead of You or lag behind You; instead, encourage and enable My Husband to walk steadily in tandem with You.
In Jesus' name I pray, Amen.

* * *

Your word is a lamp to guide my feet and a light for my path.
Psalm 119:105

DAY 38

Dear God,

Success requires that we genuinely walk in spiritual authority and You have empowered My Husband. Give him the assurance to know that You have given him the tools and ability to cover our family, relationships, finances, health, and mind. Keep his hands productive and his mind filled with divinely inspired ideas. In Jesus' name I pray, Amen.

• • •

Do not act thoughtlessly but understand what the Lord wants you to do.
Ephesians 5:17

DAY 39

Dear God,

Place a desire and determination in My Husband to pay attention to and follow your commands so that he will always be at the top and never at the bottom. Keep him at the head and not the tail and rain down blessings on the work of My Husband's hands. In Jesus' name I pray, Amen.

* * *

The Lord will send rain at the proper time from his rich treasury in the heavens and will bless all the work you do. You will lend to many nations, but you will never need to borrow from them. If you listen to these commands of the Lord your God that I am giving you today, and if you carefully obey them, the Lord will make you head and not the tail, and you will always be on top and never at the bottom.
Deuteronomy 28:12-13

DAY 40

Dear God,

Thank You for doing a great work in My Husband. Keep My Husband's mind steadfast, focused, and settled on You so that he can experience perfect peace. Deliver him from any thoughts of worry. Break patterns of insecurity and inferiority as he places his trust in You.
In Jesus' name I pray, Amen.

• • •

You will keep in perfect peace all who trust you, all whose thoughts are fixed on you!
Isaiah 26:3

FOCUS

DAY 41

Dear God,

Bringing your kingdom is our priority. Help My Husband press toward his purpose and calling and to look to You as he keeps a focus on the goal You set before him. Help My Husband to follow hard after You. Let your Will be done in and through him.
In Jesus' name I pray, Amen.

• • •

The Spirit alone gives eternal life. Human effort accomplishes nothing. And the very words I have spoken to you are spirit and life.
John 6:63

DAY 42

Dear God,

We know that prayer is essential. Teach us to pray hard and long. Help My Husband's mindset and beliefs to align with his words and behaviors. Take his thoughts to the next level to the creation of witty ideas and innovative inventions. Help him practice thinking in terms of possibilities and to believe the best. Give My Husband heavenly ambitions and the discipline to see them through. Show your answers and bless the things My Husband sets his hands to do. In Jesus' name I pray, Amen.

• • •

Put on salvation as your helmet, and take the sword of the Spirit which is the word of God. Always pray in the Spirit and on every occasion. Stay alert and be persistent in your prayers for all believers everywhere.
Ephesians 6:17-18

DAY 43

Dear God,

We know that your Will and your ways take precedence over ours. I pray that My Husband will fulfill every plan, level of success, thought, idea, goal, ambition, and dream that has been planted in him by You.
In Jesus' name I pray, Amen.

• • •

Seek the Kingdom of God above all else, and live righteously, and he will give you everything you need.
Matthew 6:33

DAY 44

Dear God,

We know that nothing is impossible with You; therefore, we will not limit what You can do through us. Lord, free My Husband's mind, and heart to dream. Transform his dreams to intentions. Then, align his actions and words so that he may stay on course to receive your desires for his life.
In Jesus' name I pray, Amen.

• • •

The Lord will work out his plans for my life—for your faithful love, O Lord, endures forever. Do not abandon me, for you made me.
Psalm 138:8

FOCUS

DAY 45

Dear God,

Take authority of My Husband's day so that he will run this race with confidence. We know that My Husband is equipped to achieve his goals, so I command this day to fully cooperate with him. I call on all the resources from heaven that You have set aside for him. I pray My Husband will not tire, trip, or fall. I pray he will not just survive but thrive. And I pray that My Husband will finish well.
In Jesus' name I pray, Amen.

* * *

Don't you realize that in a race everyone runs, but only one person gets the prize? So, run to win!
1 Corinthians 9:24

DAY 46

Dear God,

Today I ask You to keep My Husband focused only on things that will preserve his integrity and his life—mentally, physically, and spiritually. In Jesus' name I pray, Amen.

• • •

Turn my eyes from worthless things and give me life through your word.
Psalm 119:37

Focus

DAY 47

Dear God,

Help My Husband to walk in sensitivity to your Spirit. Keep his life on course and never let him compromise or settle for anything less than your best. In Jesus' name I pray, Amen.

• • •

Seek the Kingdom of God above all else, and live righteously, and he will give you everything you need.
Matthew 6:33

DAY 48

Dear God,

Help My Husband to fix his eyes straight ahead on what You have called him to be and to do. Enable My Husband to focus solely on the path You have mapped out for him. In Jesus' name I pray, Amen.

• • •

Look straight ahead and fix your eyes on what lies before you.
Proverbs 4:25

FOCUS

DAY 49

Dear God,

Teach My Husband to pray with force and perseverance. Help him to stay vigilantly and relentlessly focused on seeking You. May he begin to have undistracted and undeterred prayer. In Jesus' name I pray, Amen.

• • •

But we are not like those who turn away from God to their own destruction. We are the faithful ones, whose souls will be saved.
Hebrews 10:39

DAY 50

Dear God,

Shift the atmosphere around My Husband to be filled with the glory of God. I pray that the ministry and business that You have given My Husband thrive and that he uses them to advance your kingdom. In Jesus' name I pray, Amen.

• • •

For the Kingdom of God is not just a lot of talk; it is living by God's power.
1 Corinthians 4:20

DAY 51

Dear God,

I pray for an upgrading of My Husband's thought processes. I declare that new cycles of victory, success, and prosperity are established in his life. Everything prepared for My Husband before the foundation of the world must be released.
In Jesus' name I pray, Amen.

• • •

And it is impossible to please God without faith. Anyone who wants to come to him must believe that God exists and that he rewards those who sincerely seek him.
Hebrews 11:6

DAY 52

Dear God,

Give My Husband true vision to see the possibilities You see. Cause his spiritual eyes to function with 20/20 vision for the correct insight, understanding, and interpretations of your will. In Jesus' name I pray, Amen.

• • •

When people do not accept divine guidance, they run wild. But whoever obeys the law is joyful.
Proverbs 29:18

FOCUS

DAY 53

Dear God,

My Husband is who You say he is and can accomplish what You say he can. I pray that You sharpen My Husband's spiritual discernment so that he may hear You more clearly. Dismantle anything working to frustrate his assignment and give him prophetic insight, wisdom, and direction today. In Jesus' name I pray, Amen.

* * *

Do not copy the behavior and customs of this world, but let God transform you into a new person by changing the way you think. Then you will learn to know God's will for you, which is good and pleasing and perfect.
Romans 12:2

DAY 54

Dear God,

We choose to think big and expect great things for our future. I pray that My Husband think like Abraham—that My Husband thinks intentionally, generationally, and globally.
In Jesus' name I pray, Amen.

• • •

Let the wise listen to these proverbs and become even wiser. Let those with understanding receive guidance
Proverbs 1:5

DAY 55

Dear God,

Help My Husband to keep his focus on You in the face of trials, for You are greater than any challenge he will ever face. Let My Husband's words, thoughts, and actions all reflect his total faith and expectations of You. In Jesus' name I pray, Amen.

• • •

But when you ask him, be sure that your faith is in God alone. Do not waver, for a person with divided loyalty is as unsettled as a wave of the sea that is blown and tossed by the wind.
James 1:6

DAY 56

Dear God,

We align our words with your Word and our will with your will. I pray today that My Husband's vision is clear, and his mission is unobstructed. I pray that your power manifest in his life. Thank You for the marvelous things You are doing and will continue to do in My Husband's life. In Jesus' name I pray, Amen.

• • •

By faith we understand that the entire universe was formed at God's command, that what we now see did not come from anything that can be seen.
Hebrews 11:3

FOCUS

DAY 57

Dear God,

I pray that My Husband will meditate on your Word day and night. Bring certain verses and passages to My Husband's mind throughout the day so that he can always remember your plans for him. Thank You in advance that My Husband will prosper and succeed as he applies what he studies in your Word.
In Jesus' name I pray, Amen.

• • •

Study this Book of Instruction continually. Meditate on it day and night so you will be sure to obey everything written in it. Only then will you prosper and succeed in all you do.
Joshua 1:8

DAY 58

Dear God,

I pray that My Husband is not distracted by insignificant things. May he find strength and focus while meditating on your goodness and love.
In Jesus' name I pray, Amen.

• • •

For God is not a God of disorder but of peace, as in all the meetings of God's holy people.
1 Corinthians 14:33

DAY 59

Dear God,

Anoint My Husband's ears to hear your voice with clarity and his eyes to see things as You see them. In Jesus' name I pray, Amen.

• • •

Trust in the Lord with all your heart; do not depend on your own understanding. Seek His will in all you do, and He will show you which path to take.
Proverbs 3:5-6

DAY 60

Dear God,

I pray that My Husband keeps his focus on the goal You set before him. I pray that his thoughts are governed only by "things true, noble, reputable, authentic, compelling, gracious—the best, not the worst; the beautiful, not the ugly; things to praise, not things to curse". In Jesus' name I pray, Amen.

• • •

And now, dear brothers and sisters, one final thing. Fix your thoughts on what is true, and honorable, and right, and pure, and lovely, and admirable. Think about things that are excellent and worthy of praise. Keep putting into practice all you learned and received from me—everything you heard from me and saw me doing. Then the God of peace will be with you.
Philippians 4:8-9

FOCUS

Thanksgiving

DAY 61

Dear God,

I am glad that My Husband follows You. Thank You that he is quick to listen, slow to speak, and slow to become angry. I pray he continues to lead with his ears and follow with his mouth.
In Jesus' name I pray, Amen.

• • •

Understand this, my dear brothers, and sisters: You must all be quick to listen, slow to speak, and slow to get angry.
James 1:19

DAY 62

Dear God,

Thank You that My Husband is a hard worker. Because of this your Word says he will prosper and will be rewarded for his labor. Help him to set healthy boundaries and goals and show him proper balance.
In Jesus' name I pray, Amen.

• • •

Lazy people want much but get little,
but those who work hard will prosper.
Proverbs 13:4

THANKSGIVING

DAY 63

Dear God,

Thank You for teaching us to know your voice. Teach My Husband how to communicate with You freely and open all access to bring about clear communication from your Spirit to My Husband's mind. We want You to have unrestricted access to his mind, soul, and spirit. In Jesus' name I pray, Amen.

• • •

My sheep listen to my voice; I know them, and they follow me.
John 10:27

DAY 64

Dear God,

Thank You for daily instruction. Help My Husband to maintain constant communication with You about every detail of what needs to be done each day. Open his spirit to your instruction so that there are no interferences. Have daily (and even hourly) meetings with My Husband so that he can accomplish the impossible. In Jesus' name I pray, Amen.

• • •

Instead, we will speak the truth in love, growing in every way more and more like Christ, who is the head of his body, the church.
Ephesians 4:15

DAY 65

Dear God,

Thank You for hearing and answering our prayers. I pray that the lines of communication between My Husband and You are opened so that he can receive from heaven without interference. Help his motive in prayer only be to glorify and magnify You. All the answers he needs are found in You.
In Jesus' name I pray, Amen.

* * *

And we are confident that he hears us whenever we ask for anything that pleases him. And since we know he hears us when we make our requests, we also know that he will give us what we ask for.
1 John 5:14-15

DAY 66

Dear God,

Thank You for being a God who hears and answers prayer. We stand today as more than conquerors and declare that your plans will be made manifest in our lives. Take the limits off My Husband's thinking and let your kingdom agenda advance him into new territory. In Jesus' name I pray, Amen.

• • •

Ask me and I will tell you remarkable secrets you do not know about things to come.
Jeremiah 33:3

THANKSGIVING

DAY 67

Dear God,

It is our privilege to be part of your plans and to learn your will. Perform your "greater works" through My Husband. Help him to fulfill his calling so that the earth will be filled with your glory.
In Jesus' name I pray, Amen.

• • •

Because of Christ and our faith in him, we can now come boldly and confidently into God's presence.
Ephesians 3:12

DAY 68

Dear God,

You are concerned about every detail of our lives. So, we bring specific requests to You for a specific response. Help My Husband to have courage to bring all his requests to You because You delight in answering his prayer. May his prayers unlock heaven's vault to unleash heaven's provisions. Thank You for being so faithful to meet his needs. In Jesus' name I pray, Amen.

• • •

But if you remain in me and my words remain in you, you may ask for anything you want, and it will be granted!
John 15:7

DAY 69

Dear God,

Thank You that My Husband is not deterred by what he sees and that he persists in prayer until there is a breakthrough. In Jesus' name I pray, Amen.

• • •

Do not worry about anything; instead, pray about everything. Tell God what you need and thank him for all he has done.
Philippians 4:6

DAY 70

Dear God,

Thank You that your Word says that You have a good purpose and perfect plan for My Husband's life—a plan to prosper him and to give him hope and a future. Cause My Husband to rest knowing that You always have his best interest in mind. In Jesus' name I pray, Amen.

* * *

For I know the plans I have for you," says the Lord. "They are plans for good and not for disaster, to give you a future and a hope.
Jeremiah 29:11

THANKSGIVING

DAY 71

Dear God,

Thank You that You breathe new life into My Husband's purpose, destiny, finances, work, family, and ministry. I pray that You open the floodgates of heaven as we have faith in You. In Jesus' name I pray, Amen.

• • •

And we know that God causes everything to work together for the good of those who love God and are called according to his purpose for them.
Romans 8:28

DAY 72

Dear God,

Thank You for giving My Husband wisdom beyond his years. Surround him with strong men of God and teach him godly leadership.
In Jesus' name I pray, Amen.

• • •

As iron sharpens iron, so a
friend sharpens a friend.
Proverbs 27:17

DAY 73

Dear God,

Thank You for showing My Husband his unique purpose as he spends time in your presence. In Jesus' name I pray, Amen.

• • •

You can make many plans, but the Lord's purpose will prevail.
Proverbs 19:21

DAY 74

Dear God,

Thank You that My Husband longs to do your will. Cause him to walk in sync with your perfect timing and to praise You in advance for giving the victory. Release everything prepared for My Husband and all that You have already planned for his success.
In Jesus' name I pray, Amen.

• • •

This vision is for a future time. It describes the end, and it will be fulfilled. If it seems slow in coming, wait patiently, for it will surely take place. It will not be delayed.
Habakkuk 2:3

THANKSGIVING

DAY 75

Dear God,

Thank You that You called My Husband and You will complete the work You called him to do. Nothing is too hard for You. Even things beyond My Husband's wildest dreams are easy for You, so order his steps to fulfill your purposes. Tear down every Jericho wall so My Husband can possess the territory You have prepared for him.
In Jesus' name I pray, Amen.

• • •

We can make our plans, but the
Lord determines our steps.
Proverbs 16:9

DAY 76

Dear God,

Thank You that the effectual, fervent prayers of the righteous avail much. Guide My Husband to continue in prayer until he sees the manifestation of your promises. As he prays, release your angels to war on his behalf. Assign them to reinforce My Husband as he advances into new levels, dimensions, realms, and territories to promote and propel your kingdom. In Jesus' name I pray, Amen.

• • •

But if we look forward to something we do not yet have, we must wait patiently and confidently.
Romans 8:25

Thanksgiving

DAY 77

Dear God,

Thank You that My Husband receives favor before making any business request. Give him wisdom, courage, and full confidence, knowing that You are with him.
In Jesus' name I pray, Amen.

• • •

O Lord, please hear my prayer! Listen to the prayers of those of us who delight in honoring you. Please grant me success today by making the king favorable to me. Put it into his heart to be kind to me. In those days I was the king's cupbearer.
Nehemiah 1:11

DAY 78

Dear God,

Thank You for making My Husband the head and not the tail. Thank You that he is an industry leader, trendsetter, and an agent of change. Synchronize My Husband's actions today with heaven's rhythm so that he has the wisdom to impact his spheres of influence and transform people's lives.
In Jesus' name I pray, Amen.

• • •

And the seeds that fell on the good soil represent honest, good-hearted people who hear God's word, cling to it, and patiently produce a huge harvest.
Luke 8:15

THANKSGIVING

DAY 79

Dear God,

Thank You that everything You have for My Husband this season will come forth I declare that every invisible barrier be destroyed and that You are opening doors no man could open. May My Husband take new territory spiritually, emotionally, relationally, and professionally.
In Jesus' name I pray, Amen.

• • •

I promise you what I promised Moses: 'Wherever you set foot, you will be on land I have given you—
Joshua 1:3

DAY 80

Dear God,

Thank You for every individual and resource assigned to assist My Husband in fulfilling his kingdom assignment during this season. I declare that My Husband attracts only the things, people, and resources suitable to uphold and facilitate your plan. In Jesus' name I pray, Amen.

• • •

We can make our plans, but the
Lord determines our steps.
Proverbs 16:9

DAY 81

Dear God,

Thank You that My Husband is fearfully and wonderfully made. And thank You that My Husband is perfectly suited for his unique assignment on earth. I pray that He is filled with creativity and ingenuity today—that My Husband is a problem solver and is becoming an expert in his field. I pray that You do great and mighty things in and through him. In Jesus' name I pray, Amen.

* * *

Thank you for making me so wonderfully complex! Your workmanship is marvelous—how well I know it.
Psalm 139:14

DAY 82

Dear God,

Thank You that My Husband is a man of strong character and clear convictions. Spark his creativity and take him to spaces to find inspiration. Bring order to My Husband's environment. Let his home be filled with your peace. In Jesus' name I pray, Amen.

• • •

For we are God's masterpiece. He has created us anew in Christ Jesus, so we can do the good things he planned for us long ago.
Ephesians 2:10

THANKSGIVING

DAY 83

Dear God,

Thank You that My Husband is anointed for his assignment and that no weapon formed against him shall prosper. I pray that My Husband walks in the fullness of all You have promised.
In Jesus' name I pray, Amen.

* * *

But in that coming day no weapon turned against you will succeed. You will silence every voice raised up to accuse you. These benefits are enjoyed by the servants of the Lord; their vindication will come from me. I, the Lord, have spoken!
Isaiah 54:17

DAY 84

Dear God,

Thank You that the best is yet to come. I pray that You give My Husband new strategies for fruitfulness. In Jesus' name I pray, Amen.

• • •

Then the way you live will always honor and please the Lord, and your lives will produce every kind of good fruit. All the while, you will grow as you learn to know God better and better.
Colossians 1:10

DAY 85

Dear God,

Thank You that My Husband is an influencer and that he will leave a legacy for future generations. I pray that My Husband's destiny and speech are in sync with your Will. Prosper the work of his hands and bless our family and friends abundantly.
In Jesus' name I pray, Amen.

• • •

Commit your actions to the Lord,
and your plans will succeed.
Proverbs 16:3

DAY 86

Dear God,

Thank You for giving us absolute assurance that You are in control. I pray that My Husband greet obstacles today with rock solid faith because You hear his prayer. May he defy the status quo and walk in step with You. In Jesus' name I pray, Amen.

• • •

Faith shows the reality of what
we hope for; it is the evidence
of things we cannot see.
Hebrews 11:1

THANKSGIVING

DAY 87

Dear God,

Thank You that My Husband has the determination to base his choices on your will, your direction, and your Word. I pray that My Husband's name be associated with good things and that, in your strength, he is a blessing to his friends, family, and the next generation. In Jesus' name I pray, Amen.

• • •

That is what the Scriptures mean when they say, "No eye has seen, no ear has heard, and no mind has imagined what God has prepared for those who love him.
1 Corinthians 2:9

DAY 88

Dear God,

Thank You that My Husband is purposely built and uniquely designed by You. He is Christ's workmanship.
In Jesus' name I pray, Amen.

• • •

If you keep yourself pure, you will be a special utensil for honorable use. Your life will be clean, and you will be ready for the Master to use you for every good work.
2 Timothy 2:21

DAY 89

Dear God,

Thank You for bringing order into our lives. Where there was chaos, You brought discipline. Where there has been defeat, You brought victory. Where there had been lack, You brought abundance. You have provided all we need in life. Thank You for safely leading us.
In Jesus' name I pray, Amen.

• • •

> "I am leaving you with a gift—peace of mind and heart. And the peace I give is a gift the world cannot give. So, do not be troubled or afraid."
> John 14:27

DAY 90

Dear God,

Thank You that My Husband taps into your best by spending time with You. Speak into his life daily. Order My Husband's day as he seeks to do what You are guiding him to do.
In Jesus' name I pray, Amen.

• • •

In the night I search for you; in the morning I earnestly seek you. For only when you come to judge the earth will people learn what is right.
Isaiah 26:9

THANKSGIVING

DAY 91

Dear God,

Thank You for supplying all
My Husband's needs.
In Jesus' name I pray, Amen.

• • •

And this same God who takes care of me will
supply all your needs from his glorious riches,
which have been given to us in Christ Jesus.
Philippians 4:19

DAY 92

Dear God,

Thank You that My Husband knows your voice. And thank You that your ears are open to his prayers. Teach My Husband how to pray so that he falls into deep intercession in an instant. In Jesus' name I pray, Amen.

* * *

Always pray in the Spirit and on every occasion. Stay alert and be persistent in your prayers for all believers everywhere.
Ephesians 6:18

DAY 93

Dear God,

Thank You for speaking to My Husband. Sharpen his discernment so that he can receive directly from You. I pray that My Husband never settles for anything less than your will for his life.
In Jesus' name I pray, Amen.

• • •

Think about what I am saying. The Lord will help you understand all these things.
2 Timothy 2:7

DAY 94

Dear God,

Thank You for upgrading My Husband's speech and thoughts. And thank You for canceling the effect of negative, self-defeating words and thought processes. I declare that new cycles of victory, success, and prosperity will replace old cycles in My Husband's life today.
In Jesus' name I pray, Amen.

• • •

Do not copy the behavior and customs of this world, but let God transform you into a new person by changing the way you think. Then you will learn to know God's will for you, which is good and pleasing and perfect.
Romans 12:2

THANKSGIVING

DAY 95

Dear God,

Thank You that My Husband clings to You. I pray that in whatever pressures My Husband faces today, he remembers that You can do immeasurably more than he could ask or imagine. In Jesus' name I pray, Amen.

• • •

Now all glory to God, who is able, through his mighty power at work within us, to accomplish infinitely more than we might ask or think.
Ephesians 3:20

Humility

DAY 96

Dear God,

Keep My Husband from mistakenly believing he can handle life on his own. Prompt him to remain humble before You, learn from You, and live for You.
In Jesus' name I pray, Amen.

• • •

He leads the humble in doing right, teaching them his way.
Psalm 25:9

DAY 97

Dear God,

I pray that My Husband submits himself totally to You for he is a person of authority under authority. Lord, have the final Word and determine his steps. Lead him in the way he should go. Help him not to take one step without You. In Jesus' name I pray, Amen.

• • •

Your word is a lamp to guide my feet and a light for my path.
Psalm 119:105

HUMILITY

DAY 98

Dear God,

You have given My Husband great authority. Let him submit to You and put his trust completely in You because You are more than able to accomplish all that concerns him today. Even if he tries to make plans, You have the final say to determine his steps. Lead My Husband in the way he should go so that he will not take one step without You.
In Jesus' name I pray, Amen.

• • •

The Lord says, "I will guide you along the best pathway for your life. I will advise you and watch over you."
Psalm 32:8

DAY 99

Dear God,

I pray that My Husband will think of You throughout the day and into the night. Make his first thoughts be of You and his last thoughts before falling asleep be of You. May thoughts of You permeate his dreams.
In Jesus' name I pray, Amen.

• • •

I lie awake thinking of you, meditating on you through the night.
Psalm 63:6

DAY 100

Dear God,

We know that your thoughts are of abundance and not lack. Give My Husband divine inspirational thoughts and the ability to speak those thoughts into existence. Grow My Husband to fulfill your best plan for his life. And mature him in wisdom, authority, and supernatural ability so that he will possess his inheritance.
In Jesus' name I pray, Amen.

* * *

For the Lord grants wisdom. From his mouth comes knowledge and understanding.
Proverbs 2:6

DAY 101

Dear God,

I pray that My Husband will seek You with all his heart, not only to obtain financial success, but to know You, serve You, and live for You. Please help him see his work as a way of glorifying You and representing You in the world. Lord, bless the work of My Husband's hands today. In Jesus' name I pray, Amen.

• • •

And this same God who takes care of me will supply all your needs from his glorious riches, which have been given to us in Christ Jesus.
Philippians 4:19

HUMILITY

DAY 102

Dear God,

We know there is nothing more delightful than being with You and listening to your instruction. Teach My Husband how to be in your presence all day long. Help him to maintain an attitude of worship in every step of his day. In Jesus' name I pray, Amen.

• • •

Never stop praying.
1 Thessalonians 5:17

DAY 103

Dear God,

Even when no one is looking let our lives reflect your character. Lord, increase My Husband's knowledge of your Word and sensitivity to your voice. Help My Husband to honor You with his words and deeds so that his love for You is not compromised in any way.
In Jesus' name I pray, Amen.

• • •

The purpose of my instruction is that all believers would be filled with love that comes from a pure heart, a clear conscience, and genuine faith.
1 Timothy 1:5

DAY 104

Dear God,

Thank You for the goals and dreams You have given us in our hearts. I pray that My Husband never forget about the center—his foundation in Christ—that is the strength and source of wisdom that makes these goals and dreams possible. Continually remind My Husband today that it is all about You. You are the center of his life. Help him to work in your strength rather than through his own. In Jesus' name I pray, Amen.

• • •

Wait patiently for the Lord. Be brave and courageous. Yes, wait patiently for the Lord.
Psalm 27:14

DAY 105

Dear God,

Give My Husband a malleable heart. May he always fear You, revere You, and submit to You. In Jesus' name I pray, Amen.

• • •

Blessed are those who fear to
do wrong, but the stubborn are
headed for serious trouble.
Proverbs 28:14

HUMILITY

DAY 106

Dear God,

We will not stop praying until You answer. Help My Husband not to speak words of doubt or disbelief. When the enemy tries to discourage him, remind him that through You everything he needs is available. Have My Husband stand strong knowing that all his needs are supplied according to your riches in glory.
In Jesus' name I pray, Amen.

* * *

Do not be afraid, for I am with you. Do not be discouraged, for I am your God. I will strengthen you and help you. I will hold you up with my victorious right hand.
Isaiah 41:10

DAY 107

Dear God,

I pray My Husband will not be a proud man who pursues his own desires, but a humble man who only wants what You want. Shape him into a man after your own heart, one who kneels in total submission to your will. In Jesus' name I pray, Amen.

* * *

"Father, if you are willing, please take this cup of suffering away from me. Yet I want your will to be done, not mine."
Luke 22:42

DAY 108

Dear God,

When You call us, You supernaturally equip us with spiritual abilities in line with that divine mission and assignment. Thank You that those spiritual gifts function in My Husband's life. Thank You that he can do great things and see miracles happen. Thank You that the gifts and calling of God are irrevocable. And thank You that My Husband is not satisfied with the status quo. Give My Husband all that You have for him today. In Jesus' name I pray, Amen.

• • •

For God's gifts and his call can never be withdrawn.
Romans 11:29

DAY 109

Dear God,

Give My Husband a fresh
revelation of who he is in You
and the incredible access
he has as your child.
In Jesus' name I pray, Amen.

* * *

Then as I looked, I saw a door standing
open in heaven, and the same voice
I had heard before spoke to me
like a trumpet blast. The voice said,
"Come up here, and I will show you
what must happen after this."
Revelation 4:1

HUMILITY

DAY 110

Dear God,

Thank You that My Husband does not seek the spotlight, but that he seeks the presence of God. Take My Husband into new spiritual dimensions that he may be among those who learn your plans and release your will into the earth. Prepare his heart for the responsibility of this place in the Spirit. In Jesus' name I pray, Amen.

* * *

This vision is for a future time. It describes the end, and it will be fulfilled. If it seems slow in coming, wait patiently, for it will surely take place. It will not be delayed.
Habakkuk 2:3

DAY 111

Dear God,

Equip and empower My Husband to show that he loves You by obeying your teaching. Help him not to be proud and go his own way, but to be humble and submit to your better way.
In Jesus' name I pray, Amen.

• • •

The Lord says, "I will guide you along the best pathway for your life. I will advise you and watch over you.
Psalm 32:8

DAY 112

Dear God,

Keep My Husband from trying to do everything in his own strength. Guide him to be still, trust in your sovereign plan, and draw from your power.
In Jesus' name I pray, Amen.

• • •

Search for the Lord and for his
strength; continually seek him.
1 Chronicles 16:11

DAY 113

Dear God,

May My Husband experience a vibrant relationship with You where he humbly prays, worships, and submits to You. In Jesus' name I pray, Amen.

• • •

The one thing I ask of the Lord—the thing I seek most—is to live in the house of the Lord all the days of my life, delighting in the Lord's perfections and meditating in his Temple.
Psalm 27:4

HUMILITY

DAY 114

Dear God,

Destiny is God-given, God-revealed, and God-directed. Direct My Husband to his destiny as I pray today. Deposit your ideas into his spirit. My Husband's gifts, calling, abilities, skills, and talents are uniquely from You. I pray My Husband uses everything You have placed within his hands for your glory. In Jesus' name I pray, Amen.

• • •

May he equip you with all you need for doing his will. May he produce in you, through the power of Jesus Christ, every good thing that is pleasing to him. All glory to him forever and ever! Amen.
Joel 3:9-10

DAY 115

Dear God,

Your Word says that He who is in me is greater than he that is in the world. Lord, increase My Husband's awareness of who he is in You and what your will is for his life. I know You have already equipped My Husband to do exactly what You have called him to do. May he pursue his destiny without fear because he belongs to You and You are faithful to complete your work in him.
In Jesus' name I pray, Amen.

* * *

For God has not given us a spirit of fear and timidity, but of power, love, and self-discipline.
2 Timothy 1:7

DAY 116

Dear God,

While I pray My Husband will be successful and influential, I also pray that he will remain humble and grateful. Thank You that My Husband is not prideful about his accomplishments. And thank You for giving him the ability, providing him the opportunity, and blessing his ingenuity.
In Jesus' name I pray, Amen.

• • •

Commit your actions to the Lord,
and your plans will succeed.
Proverbs 16:3

DAY 117

Dear God,

I pray that My Husband always fears You, reveres You, and submits to You. In Jesus' name I pray, Amen.

• • •

Jesus told him, "I am the way, the truth, and the life. No one can come to the Father except through me".
John 14:6

HUMILITY

DAY 118

Dear God,

Thank You for equipping My Husband with divine thoughts and inspired words. Let My Husband's words be more than motivation; let them carry life and break through roadblocks. In Jesus' name I pray, Amen.

• • •

May the words of my mouth and the meditation of my heart be pleasing to you, O Lord, my rock, and my redeemer.
Psalm 19:14

DAY 119

Dear God,

We know that words have power, presence, and prophetic implications so we commit to having a positive mindset. I pray that You influence My Husband's thoughts so that his life and his speech reflect You. You have placed My Husband here to fulfill your purpose and You have called him to be a leader. Thank You that he bears your light.
In Jesus' name I pray, Amen.

• • •

There is more hope for a fool than for someone who speaks without thinking.
Proverbs 29:20

DAY 120

Dear God,

Empower and equip My Husband to walk by faith and not by sight. Help him to trust in, believe in, and cling to your promises even when what he sees is still lining up. May My Husband's faith in You be what guides his every step today. In Jesus' name I pray, Amen.

* * *

And now, dear brothers and sisters, one final thing. Fix your thoughts on what is true, and honorable, and right, and pure, and lovely, and admirable. Think about things that are excellent and worthy of praise.
Philippians 4:8

DAY 121

Dear God,

You are My Husband's Maker and he is under your care. Thank You that My Husband has a humble spirit to worship You and kneel in adoration before You. In Jesus' name I pray, Amen.

• • •

Jesus replied, "'You must love the Lord your God with all your heart, all your soul, and all your mind."
Matthew 22:37

HUMILITY

DAY 122

Dear God,

Thank You that My Husband is mindful of what he speaks and when he speaks it. I pray that You continue to guard his lips. Help My Husband to weigh his words wisely. In Jesus' name I pray, Amen.

• • •

Those who control their tongue will have a long life; opening your mouth can ruin everything.
Proverbs 13:3

DAY 123

Dear God,

We know that prayer changes our perception to see things from your perspective. As My Husband faces situations and decisions today, give him wisdom and revelations about the specific actions to take. Let whatever My Husband does or says prosper because of prayer. In Jesus' name I pray, Amen.

• • •

The Lord directs the steps of the godly.
He delights in every detail of their lives.
Psalm 37:23

DAY 124

Dear God,

Bless My Husband with friends who sharpen him—ones who challenge him, inspire him, and hold him accountable. Give My Husband wisdom and grace to do the same for the close friends in his life.
In Jesus' name I pray, Amen.

• • •

As iron sharpens iron, so a
friend sharpens a friend.
Proverbs 27:17

Grace

DAY 125

Dear God,

Thank You for progress in My Husband's prayer life. Reveal more of Yourself to My Husband today and dismantle any negativity working to frustrate his day.
In Jesus' name I pray, Amen.

• • •

Devote yourselves to prayer with an alert mind and a thankful heart.
Colossians 4:2

DAY 126

Dear God,

My Husband is faithful in what You have given him, so raise him up and enlarge his territory. Synchronize his actions with your will. Let My Husband be the perfect example of your love, mercy, and grace to our generation. Give him divine discipline so that everything his hands touch prospers.
In Jesus' name I pray, Amen.

• • •

"If you are faithful in little things, you will be faithful in large ones. But if you are dishonest in little things, you won't be honest with greater responsibilities."
Luke 16:10

GRACE

DAY 127

Dear God,

Help My Husband responsibly utilize the gifts You have given him to be a blessing to our family, this community, and our nation. You have divinely placed him in a position to help others accomplish their God-given dreams. Thank You that My Husband is faithful. Increase his networking abilities. Direct him to build with those who are willing and called to work beside him.
In Jesus' name I pray, Amen.

* * *

Live in harmony with each other. Do not be too proud to enjoy the company of ordinary people. And do not think you know it all!
Romans 12:16

DAY 128

Dear God,

Teach My Husband how to speak words that are full of grace and seasoned with salt—words that make others thirsty to know You more. Guide him to use speech that represents You well today. In Jesus' name I pray, Amen.

* * *

Let your conversation be gracious and attractive so that you will have the right response for everyone.
Colossians 4:6

Grace

DAY 129

Dear God,

You had a plan for My Husband before he was even born—a plan that You will fulfill. Help My Husband to be diligent so that he will receive the FULL reward You have prepared for him. Bless his hands, Lord. And let his name be associated only with good things. In Jesus' name I pray, Amen.

* * *

So, let us not get tired of doing what is good. At just the right time we will reap a harvest of blessing if we do not give up.
Galatians 6:9

DAY 130

Dear God,

Just as Joseph's master saw that You gave him success in everything he did, I pray that My Husband's colleagues, sponsors, partners, friends, and family see that You are with him—that You give him success. May My Husband find favor and recognize that favor as your blessing on his life and in his work. In Jesus' name I pray, Amen.

• • •

"For I hold you by your right hand I, the Lord your God. And I say to you, 'Don't be afraid. I am here to help you.'"
Isaiah 41:13

GRACE

DAY 131

Dear God,

I lift up My Husband's relationship with his parents. Thank You that he honors and respects his father and mother, so that he will have a long full life. Give him grace to forgive when let down and an even greater heart to appreciate them for the times they have encouraged him on. In Jesus' name I pray, Amen.

* * *

Since God chose you to be the holy people he loves, you must clothe yourselves with tenderhearted mercy, kindness, humility, gentleness, and patience.
Colossians 3:12

DAY 132

Dear God,

I pray My Husband will have great success in everything he does today. Open his eyes to see that his accomplishments and achievements are because of your blessing and presence in his life. In Jesus' name I pray, Amen.

• • •

"Be still and know that I am God! I will be honored by every nation. I will be honored throughout the world."
Psalm 46:10

DAY 133

Dear God,

Help My Husband to meditate on your Word day and night so that You will prosper him. Cancel negative, self-defeating thoughts and give My Husband a fresh mind and fresh excitement to anticipate the good things You will do.
In Jesus' name I pray, Amen.

• • •

May all my thoughts be pleasing to him, for I rejoice in the Lord.
Psalm 104:34

DAY 134

Dear God,

Just as Nehemiah prayed for a favorable response before he made his request to the king, prompt My Husband to pray to receive favor before he makes presentations or requests of others in business. Give him wisdom, courage, and strength to go about his work with confidence knowing that You are with him.
In Jesus' name I pray, Amen.

• • •

You will enjoy the fruit of your labor.
How joyful and prosperous you will be!
Psalm 128:2

GRACE

DAY 135

Dear God,

Your Word says that when two or more agree and gather in your name, that You are with them. Thank You for placing My Husband's relationships—in family and work—in perfect harmony with You. Create healthy patterns and unity in those relationships so that My Husband may walk in agreement with You and obtain new levels of passion and zeal for his calling.
In Jesus' name I pray, Amen.

* * *

"I also tell you this: If two of you agree here on earth concerning anything you ask, my Father in heaven will do it for you.
Matthew 18:19

DAY 136

Dear God,

I pray that My Husband will see good things come from the work of his hands. Let him reap in full the fruit of his labor. May he be noticed, acknowledged, and praised for a job well done. Let My Husband see the ways he has made a lasting impact on the world and in his sphere of influence.
In Jesus' name I pray, Amen.

• • •

Wise words bring many benefits, and hard work brings rewards.
Proverbs 12:14

DAY 137

Dear God,

Encourage and inspire My Husband to speak words that are wise and gracious. Keep his conversations free of destructive words and fill them with words that bring honor to You. In Jesus' name I pray, Amen.

* * *

Gentle words are a tree of life; a deceitful tongue crushes the spirit.
Proverbs 15:4

DAY 138

Dear God,

Your ways are higher than our ways and your thoughts are higher than our thoughts. They are beyond human understanding. The Bible tells us that as believers, we should have the mind of Christ. I pray that My Husband will align his thoughts with Christ's thoughts, his reasoning with Christ's reasoning, and his purposes with Christ's purposes. In Jesus' name I pray, Amen.

• • •

Do not copy the behavior and customs of this world, but let God transform you into a new person by changing the way you think. Then you will learn to know God's will for you, which is good and pleasing and perfect.
Romans 12:2

GRACE

DAY 139

Dear God,

Give My Husband the wisdom and the will to cast his concerns and worries on You once and for all. May he know without a shadow of a doubt that You care for his every need.
In Jesus' name I pray, Amen.

* * *

Give all your worries and cares to
God, for he cares about you.
1 Peter 5:7

DAY 140

Dear God,

Use My Husband to establish your righteousness today. Cause the spiritual atmosphere to shift and become conducive around him. Let him walk before You with integrity, honoring You with his words and his actions. I declare that My Husband's name be associated with honesty, humility, grace, joy, peace, generosity, and wisdom. In Jesus' name I pray, Amen.

• • •

For God is working in you, giving you the desire and the power to do what pleases him.
Philippians 2:13

Grace

DAY 141

Dear God,

Thank You for your glorious power that is displayed in My Husband's life. When he feels weak or tired, help him to remember that your grace is sufficient and that your strength is enough to get him through any struggle, over any hurdle, and around any roadblock. In Jesus' name I pray, Amen.

• • •

Each time he said, "My grace is all you need. My power works best in weakness." So now I am glad to boast about my weaknesses, so that the power of Christ can work through me.
2 Corinthians 12:9

DAY 142

Dear God,

What we think has the power to transform our lives. So, I speak life and truth over My Husband today. Fill My Husband's mind with good, great, and godly thoughts. Give him a sensitivity and obedience to your voice. In Jesus' name I pray, Amen.

• • •

And now, dear brothers and sisters, one final thing. Fix your thoughts on what is true, and honorable, and right, and pure, and lovely, and admirable. Think about things that are excellent and worthy of praise.
Philippians 4:8

GRACE

DAY 143

Dear God,

Stretch My Husband. Transform his mind. Increase his paradigm of success and prosperity beyond this realm. And enlarge My Husband's understanding of your will so that he has the disciples' anointing for learning on him today.
In Jesus' name I pray, Amen.

* * *

So, faith comes from hearing, that is, hearing the Good News about Christ.
Romans 10:17

DAY 144

Dear God,

Eyes have not seen nor ears heard the things You have prepared for us. Show My Husband how to unlock your secrets for him. And as My Husband follows your instructions, I pray that new possibilities unfold today.
In Jesus' name I pray, Amen.

• • •

I will hurry, without delay, to obey your commands.
Psalm 119:60

DAY 145

Dear God,

I believe You have designed My Husband to be a success and to prosper physically, financially, relationally, socially, spiritually, and in every other way a person can prosper. I pray that My Husband has an excellent spirit and does not procrastinate. He is an influencer and he leaves a legacy for the next generation. I pray that My Husband's environment is healthy and that he will live authentically to accomplish all he was born to do. In Jesus' name I pray, Amen.

• • •

You will keep in perfect peace all who trust in you, all whose thoughts are fixed on you!
Isaiah 26:3

DAY 146

Dear God,

You have given My Husband all that he needs to meet the challenges of life. Move My Husband to plug into your power and to access your strength today.
In Jesus' name I pray, Amen.

• • •

For I can do everything through Christ, who gives me strength.
Philippians 4:13

GRACE

DAY 147

Dear God,

Thank You that we can do all things through You. Let My Husband be more aware of your presence and power in his life today. I pray that his environment is prosperous, our family is blessed, and all his needs are supplied according to your riches in glory. Let joy, peace, prosperity, and success be abundant in his life. I pray that your blessings make My Husband rich, and that everything he needs to fulfill his destiny be placed at his disposal when needed. In Jesus' name I pray, Amen.

* * *

"Yes, I am the vine; you are the branches.
Those who remain in me, and I in them,
will produce much fruit. For apart
from me you can do nothing."
John 15:5

DAY 148

Dear God,

We come into agreement with what You have already said. I pray that My Husband fills his mind with your Word and fills his atmosphere with your promises on every matter. Order My Husband's steps so he will not stumble or fall.
In Jesus' name I pray, Amen.

• • •

Let us hold tightly without wavering to the hope we affirm, for God can be trusted to keep his promise.
Hebrews 10:23

DAY 149

Dear God,

I lift up My Husband's relationship with his parents. May My Husband value their investment in his life. In Jesus' name I pray, Amen.

• • •

"Honor your father and mother, as the Lord your God commanded you. Then you will live a long, full life in the land the Lord your God is giving you."
Deuteronomy 5:16

DAY 150

Dear God,

Thank You that your plans for My Husband will always prevail. I pray that the angels assigned to My Husband reinforce him as he is an agent of change in this world. Anoint My Husband to advance into new levels, dimensions, realms, and territories.
In Jesus' name I pray, Amen.

• • •

> For he will order his angels to
> protect you wherever you go.
> Psalm 91:11

GRACE

DAY 151

Dear God,

I speak light into My Husband's family, his relationships, his finances, his health, and his mind. Fill My Husband's mind with divinely inspired ideas. Give him the tools and ability to take new territory where his hands are productive, and where he makes history in this world. I pray that My Husband is empowered to become all that he was born to be. In Jesus' name I pray, Amen.

• • •

Commit your actions to the Lord, and your plans will succeed.
Proverbs 16:3

Wisdom

DAY 152

Dear God,

When My Husband has a decision to make, direct him to astute men who can provide wise counsel. In Jesus' name I pray, Amen.

• • •

Get all the advice and instruction you can, so you will be wise the rest of your life. You can make many plans, but the Lord's purpose will prevail.
Proverbs 19:20-21

DAY 153

Dear God,

When My Husband must make a decision today, I pray he will weigh his options on the scale of your Word. Give him understanding so he will know the right path to take and the best choice to make. In Jesus' name I pray, Amen.

• • •

Give me understanding and I will obey your instructions; I will put them into practice with all my heart.
Psalm 119:34

WISDOM

DAY 154

Dear God,

Stir up a desire in My Husband to seek your wisdom for every decision he makes. Give him direction for every choice he makes. I pray he will not depend on worldly knowledge, but on your infinite wisdom which knows no bounds. In Jesus' name I pray, Amen.

• • •

Joyful is the person who finds wisdom, the one who gains understanding. For wisdom is more profitable than silver, and her wages are better than gold. Wisdom is more precious than rubies; nothing you desire can compare with her. If you need wisdom, ask our generous God, and he will give it to you. He will not rebuke you for asking.
Proverbs 3:13-15

DAY 155

Dear God,

Fill My Husband with wisdom and understanding so that he can make the best decisions possible. Cultivate in him a desire for godly wisdom over earthly treasures. And help My Husband to discipline his life so that he may sustain high levels of success and accomplishment for the kingdom of God.
In Jesus' name I pray, Amen.

• • •

If you need wisdom, ask our generous God, and he will give it to you. He will not rebuke you for asking.
James 1:5

DAY 156

Dear God,

Just as You gave Daniel wisdom to make the best decisions, I ask You to give My Husband your wisdom to make the best decisions. Bless him with supernatural knowledge and spot-on discernment for every choice he makes today. In Jesus' name I pray, Amen.

* * *

Let the message about Christ, in all its richness, fill your lives. Teach and counsel each other with all the wisdom he gives. Sing psalms and hymns and spiritual songs to God with thankful hearts.
Colossians 3:16

DAY 157

Dear God,

Give My Husband the spirit of wisdom and revelation so that he may know You better. Enlighten his mind so that he will know You intellectually, personally, intimately, and experientially. In Jesus' name I pray, Amen.

• • •

Asking God, the glorious Father of our Lord Jesus Christ, to give you spiritual wisdom and insight so that you might grow in your knowledge of God.
Ephesians 1:17

WISDOM

DAY 158

Dear God,

Reveal to us supernatural strategies for success, spiritual growth, good health, and prosperity. Give My Husband wisdom on how to conduct his businesses, how to invest and manage money, what he needs to do to nurture relationships, and how to discipline himself to keep his body fit and strong. Show him new ways of living and upgrade his thinking to accomplish your will. Finally, prepare My Husband to receive the supernatural discipline to implement your kingdom methods today. In Jesus' name I pray, Amen.

* * *

And though you started with little,
you will end with much.
Job 8:7

DAY 159

Dear God,

You are near to everyone who calls on You, so I know You are near My Husband today. As he seeks the wisdom of heaven, teach My Husband how to live, to pray, and to walk in sync with your perfect timing. In Jesus' name I pray, Amen.

• • •

God saved you by his grace when you believed. And you cannot take credit for this; it is a gift from God.
Ephesians 2:8

DAY 160

Dear God,

I pray You will fill My Husband's mind with the knowledge of your will. Give him spiritual wisdom and understanding that go beyond human explanation and earthly education. Make the Scripture come alive for My Husband, so that he will grasp insights that he has never understood.
In Jesus' name I pray, Amen.

• • •

So, we have not stopped praying for you since we first heard about you. We ask God to give you complete knowledge of his will and to give you spiritual wisdom and understanding.
Colossians 1:9

DAY 161

Dear God,

Illuminate your Word. Give My Husband a spirit of wisdom and revelation. Place your anointing upon him. Place on him Solomon's anointing for resource management, wisdom, wealth, success, and prosperity; Isaac's anointing for investment strategies; Cyrus' anointing for financial acumen; And Daniel's anointing for government, excellence, and integrity. Let the anointing on My Husband's life flow unhindered and attract only those divinely ordained to assist him in fulfilling his assignment. In Jesus' name I pray, Amen.

• • •

But you are not like that, for the
Holy One has given you his Spirit,
and all of you know the truth.
1 John 2:20

WISDOM

DAY 162

Dear God,

Thank You that My Husband makes your commands the guiding principles of his life. In Jesus' name I pray, Amen.

• • •

The commandments of the Lord are right, bringing joy to the heart. The commands of the Lord are clear, giving insight for the living.
Psalm 19:8

DAY 163

Dear God,

I pray that My Husband walks in sync with You. Give him your divine instruction so that he will know exactly which way to go. Have your Word renew his mind daily so that your light will shine through him today.
In Jesus' name I pray, Amen.

• • •

He renews my strength. He guides me along right paths, bringing honor to his name.
Psalm 23:3

DAY 164

Dear God,

We know that You have already released every possibility for our lives. So, we expect that everything we pray for, will manifest. I declare today that only your plans will prevail in My Husband's life. Give My Husband the wisdom, knowledge, and understanding he needs to honor You today. Remind him in a unique way that everything he desires is already sealed in the Spirit realm. In Jesus' name I pray, Amen.

• • •

You will succeed in whatever you choose to do, and light will shine on the road ahead of you.
Job 22:28

DAY 165

Dear God,

Thank You that My Husband's desires look like Yours. Remind My Husband that as he spends more time with You, You do not just give him what he wants; rather You will make him desire what You want. In Jesus' name I pray, Amen.

• • •

Take delight in the Lord, and he will give you your heart's desires. Commit everything you do to the Lord. Trust him, and he will help you.
Psalm 37:4-5

WISDOM

DAY 166

Dear God,

Open My Husband's eyes to recognize your goodness throughout his day. Let him see You in moments of sudden glory where You make your presence known.
In Jesus' name I pray, Amen.

* * *

Surely your goodness and unfailing love will pursue me all the days of my life, and I will live in the house of the Lord forever.
Psalm 27:24

DAY 167

Dear God,

Place within My Husband a teachable spirit. Help him commit to seek your guidance in every endeavor before doing anything else.
In Jesus' name I pray, Amen.

• • •

The Lord directs our steps, so why try to understand everything along the way?
Proverbs 20:24

DAY 168

Dear God,

Help us to spend more time with our physical eyes closed and our spiritual eyes open. Show My Husband What You really want for him and the plans You have for him to impact this world. Give My Husband a clear vision. Remind him of what really matters to You so that he will become all he was born to be.
In Jesus' name I pray, Amen.

• • •

Open my eyes to see the wonderful
truths in your instructions.
Psalm 119:18

DAY 169

Dear God,

Your plans are so great that we cannot comprehend all You have prepared. What You want for My Husband's life is too big for him to manage on his own. He needs You! Order My Husband's steps according to your Word. In Jesus' name I pray, Amen.

• • •

We can make our plans, but the
Lord determines our steps.
Proverbs 16:9

WISDOM

DAY 170

Dear God,

I ask that You open My Husband's eyes to see the many ways You have provided for his needs. Please do not let him miss your blessings that are right there for the taking.
In Jesus' name I pray, Amen.

• • •

Whatever is good and perfect is a gift coming down to us from God our Father, who created all the lights in the heavens. He never changes or casts a shifting shadow.
James 1:17

DAY 171

Dear God,

Download into My Husband's spirit your divine strategies and wisdom. Enable My Husband to walk out your plans on this earth and accomplish your purpose and calling for his life. And as he yields to your plans and purposes, use My Husband to touch others' lives. In Jesus' name I pray, Amen.

• • •

Indeed, the Sovereign Lord never does anything until he reveals his plans to his servants the prophets.
Amos 3:7

DAY 172

Dear God,

We will not get ahead of You today. May My Husband listen for the intelligence that comes from your throne room so that his prayers are strategic and prophetically aligned to bring breakthrough. In Jesus' name I pray, Amen.

• • •

That is why we never give up. Though our bodies are dying, our spirits are being renewed every day.
2 Corinthians 4:16

DAY 173

Dear God,

Meeting with You today is our priority. Help My Husband to get your plan and then set his agenda around it. Let nothing on his agenda today be more important than You. In Jesus' name I pray, Amen.

• • •

I love all who love me. Those who search will surely find me.
Proverbs 8:17

WISDOM

DAY 174

Dear God,

Order My Husband's steps in your Word and guide him into all truth. Let your Word renew My Husband's mind and change his perspective. Then, let the rest of his life fall in line so he exemplifies the fruit of your Spirit. As My Husband diligently seeks You and studies your Word, transform his life and prayers. Help My Husband to listen more and wait for revelation from your throne so his prayers will be strategic and effective. In Jesus' name I pray, Amen.

• • •

For everything there is a season, a time for every activity under heaven.
Ecclesiastes 3:1

DAY 175

Dear God,

Help us to pray correctly, consistently, thankfully, and persistently so that we will know exactly what to do to fulfill your purpose and maximize our potential. I pray that your line of communication with My Husband is cleared so You have unrestricted access to his mind and spirit.
In Jesus' name I pray, Amen.

• • •

For everything comes from him and exists by his power and is intended for his glory. All glory to him forever! Amen.
Romans 11:36

DAY 176

Dear God,

Open My Husband's eyes so that he recognizes your presence and workings in his life. As he moves today, heighten his sensitivity to your glory surrounding him.
In Jesus' name I pray, Amen.

• • •

What is more, I am with you, and I will protect you wherever you go. One day I will bring you back to this land. I will not leave you until I have finished giving you everything I have promised you."
Genesis 28:15

DAY 177

Dear God,

We limit ourselves when we rely on our own wisdom. As My Husband makes his plans and decisions, I pray that You determine each of his steps today. In Jesus' name I pray, Amen.

• • •

We can make our plans, but the Lord determines our steps.
Proverbs 16:9

WISDOM

DAY 178

Dear God,

Remind My Husband of the dreams You placed into his heart. Guide My Husband as he breathes new life into his vision, his strategies, and his alliances. I pray that My Husband's best days are just ahead. In Jesus' name I pray, Amen.

• • •

Such knowledge is too wonderful for me, too great for me to understand!
Psalm 139:6

DAY 179

Dear God,

Thank You for supplying all My Husband's needs. Teach My Husband and instruct him in the way he should go. I pray that My Husband commits to your plan and is encouraged today to accomplish what he was born to do.
In Jesus' name I pray, Amen.

• • •

For I know the plans I have for you," says the Lord. "They are plans for good and not for disaster, to give you a future and a hope.
Jeremiah 29:11

DAY 180

Dear God,

We do not take lightly the power of our words. I speak light and life into My Husband's day. Illuminate the path You would have him to walk. I pray that My Husband maximizes his potential today as he moves boldly toward his destiny. Guide My Husband and bring insight and understanding that will cause him to be more productive.
In Jesus' name I pray, Amen.

* * *

The Lord will work out his plans for my life—for your faithful love, O Lord, endures forever. Do not abandon me, for you made me.
Psalm 138:8

DAY 181

Dear God,

We know that we are called into ministry. You are the potter and we are the clay. Thank You for giving My Husband the gifts and abilities he has. You know best how he should use them. Train his ears to hear your voice and guide him in the way he should go. Make all My Husband's ways prosperous. In Jesus' name I pray, Amen.

• • •

But if you remain in me and my words remain in you, you may ask for anything you want, and it will be granted! When you produce much fruit, you are my true disciples. This brings great glory to my Father.
John 15:7-8

WISDOM

Protection

DAY 182

Dear God,

Thank You for the gift of your peace which transcends all understanding. May it guard and protect My Husband's heart. I ask You to keep his heart under surveillance of your all-seeing eye and in your protective care.
In Jesus' name I pray, Amen.

• • •

Then you will experience God's peace, which exceeds anything we can understand. His peace will guard your hearts and minds as you live in Christ Jesus.
Philippians 4:7

DAY 183

Dear God,

Protect My Husband's mind because every spiritual battle is won or lost at the threshold of the mind. Help him recognize the devil's lies quickly, reject them completely, and replace them with your Word.
In Jesus' name I pray, Amen.

• • •

For we are not fighting against flesh-and-blood enemies, but against evil rulers and authorities of the unseen world, against mighty powers in this dark world, and against evil spirits in the heavenly places.
Ephesians 6:12-13

PROTECTION

DAY 184

Dear God,

Let the words of My Husband's mouth and the meditation of his heart be acceptable in your sight. I pray that My Husband does not fear new territory because You have called him to influence others. Help him to not second-guess what You have said, but to commit to bear your light as a change agent in the world. In Jesus' name I pray, Amen.

* * *

Commit everything you do to the Lord.
Trust him, and he will help you.
Psalm 37:5

DAY 185

Dear God,

Just as You protected David from the paw of the lion, the paw of the bear, and the threats of Goliath, I pray You will protect My Husband from those who would rise up in any battle You have called him to face. Help him not be afraid of those who appear seemingly more powerful than him, but to be confident in your all-encompassing protection and all-sufficient power. In Jesus' name I pray, Amen.

• • •

But the Lord is faithful; he will strengthen you and guard you from the evil one.
2 Thessalonians 3:3

DAY 186

Dear God,

Thank You for placing your anointing on My Husband. I pray that the plans and purpose of your Will prevail in his life. Assign angels to reinforce My Husband as he advances into new levels dimensions, realms, and territories. Lord, make My Husband your ambassador on earth as he commits to be an agent of change in the world.
In Jesus' name I pray, Amen.

• • •

In the same way, let your good deeds shine out for all to see, so that everyone will praise your heavenly Father.
Matthew 5:16

DAY 187

Dear God,

Just as the warring angles surrounded and protected the prophet Elisha, I pray My Husband will be confident that your power surrounding him is greater than anyone or anything he faces. Even though he may not see it, reassure My Husband that he is always under your guiding and protective care. In Jesus' name I pray, Amen.

• • •

The name of the Lord is a strong fortress;
the godly run to him and are safe.
Proverbs 18:10

PROTECTION

DAY 188

Dear God,

We want all You have for us so show us in prayer how to keep our spiritual eyes open for understanding. Give My Husband divine insights, revelations, creative ideas, and cutting-edge concepts for his work. Remove any doubt that could keep him from trusting the prophetic visions You have already shown him. And Lord send angels to protect My Husband and reassure him of your plans and his purpose.
In Jesus' name I pray, Amen.

* * *

I tell you, you can pray for anything,
and if you believe that you have
received it, it will be yours.
Mark 11:24

DAY 189

Dear God,

Thank You for being the Great Shepherd who leads, protects, and cares for us. Remind My Husband that because You are his Shepherd, he has everything he needs.
In Jesus' name I pray, Amen.

• • •

The Lord is my shepherd; I have all that I need.
Psalm 23:1

DAY 190

Dear God,

I pray for a hedge of protection around My Husband and everything he has today. Surround him on all sides with your protective presence and keep him under your care.
In Jesus' name I pray, Amen.

• • •

You have always put a wall of protection around him and his home and his property. You have made him prosper in everything he does. Look how rich he is!
Job 1:10

DAY 191

Dear God,

May your favor be all over
My Husband today. Establish
the work of his hands and
give him great success.
In Jesus' name I pray, Amen.

• • •

And may the Lord our God show us his
approval and make our efforts successful.
Yes, make our efforts successful!
Psalm 90:17

PROTECTION

DAY 192

Dear God,

Give My Husband a desire to seek your wisdom and understanding in every decision he makes today. Interrupt his agenda and place the anointing of prayer warrior on him. Give him the words to say, ears to hear, and a heart to feel those in need. In Jesus' name I pray, Amen.

* * *

Finally, all of you should be of one mind. Sympathize with each other. Love each other as brothers and sisters. Be tenderhearted and keep a humble attitude.
1 Peter 3:8

DAY 193

Dear God,

Thank You for being My Husband's rock and fortress in whom he can take refuge. I pray You will shield him from harm and protect him from evil. Lord, have My Husband's back today. In Jesus' name I pray, Amen.

• • •

The Lord is my rock, my fortress, and my savior; my God is my rock, in whom I find protection. He is my shield, the power that saves me, and my place of safety. I called on the Lord, who is worthy of praise, and he saved me from my enemies.
Psalm 18:2-3

DAY 194

Dear God,

My Husband is ready to step into his destiny. He was born within this generation to contribute something significant and to fulfill your purpose. I pray that You remove anyone who tries to kill his dreams or fill his mind with doubt and intimidation. Be with My Husband in his business dealings, negotiations, and communications today.
In Jesus' name I pray, Amen.

• • •

"I have told you all this so that you may have peace in me. Here on earth you will have many trials and sorrows. But take heart because I have overcome the world."
John 16:33

DAY 195

Dear God,

Thank You that all My Husband's God-given goals are achievable. Fill him with courage to impact every sphere of his influence and increase his ability to make a difference in this world. May he hold nothing back from his service to your kingdom. In Jesus' name I pray, Amen.

• • •

This is my command—be strong and courageous! Do not be afraid or discouraged. For the Lord, your God is with you wherever you go."
Joshua 1:9

PROTECTION

DAY 196

Dear God,

I pray that My Husband finds favor today with his partners and anyone who has authority to make provisions for his work. Meet My Husband's needs; supply the means beforehand. Mark his conversations with grace and wisdom so that his endeavors are fruitful. Give him more than enough today.
In Jesus' name I pray, Amen.

• • •

And God will generously provide all you need.
Then you will always have everything you
need, and plenty left over to share with others.
2 Corinthians 9:8

DAY 197

Dear God,

Thank You that My Husband values his relationship with You and that nothing can separate him from your love. Show My Husband what is best for him. Help him make the best decisions possible. Protect him from harmful decisions and lead him toward helpful choices. In Jesus' name I pray, Amen.

• • •

For you are my hiding place; you protect me from trouble. You surround me with songs of victory.
Psalm 32:7

DAY 198

Dear God,

We ask You for wisdom. Open My Husband's eyes and ears to the things of the Spirit. Protect him from spiritual blindness and deafness. Give My Husband divine understanding of time and season so he will know exactly how to pray. May he grow in You.
In Jesus' name I pray, Amen.

* * *

For everything there is a season, a time
for every activity under heaven.
Ecclesiastes 3:1

DAY 199

Dear God,

Purify our hearts and remove every hindrance that would keep us from hearing You clearly today. Help My Husband to be stronger in the fruits and gifts of the Spirit so he can meet the needs of others that come to him. Direct My Husband so he will know what to say and do. In Jesus' name I pray, Amen.

• • •

Joyful is the person who finds wisdom, the one who gains understanding. For wisdom is more profitable than silver, and her wages are better than gold. For everything there is a season, a time for every activity under heaven.
Proverbs 3:13–14

PROTECTION

DAY 200

Dear God,

The supernatural realm is where change happens. Cause the supernatural realm to become more real to us than the natural. Allow My Husband to tap into the frequency of heaven and receive your instructions on how to pray. We know that whatever is loosed in heaven will be loosed on earth, so we command the enemy to release everything he has illegally held up and held back. The enemy must let go of everything that belongs to My Husband in Jesus' name. I declare that My Husband will fulfill the mission You have for him today without hindrance. May he have everything he needs to accomplish your Will. In Jesus' name I pray, Amen.

* * *

Now all glory to God, who is able, through his mighty power at work within us, to accomplish infinitely more than we might ask or think.
Ephesians 3:20

DAY 201

Dear God,

Protect My Husband's thoughts and decision-making. Give him understanding so that he may clearly comprehend what You want him to do and how You want him to do it. In Jesus' name I pray, Amen.

• • •

Do not act thoughtlessly but understand what the Lord wants you to do.
Ephesians 5:17

DAY 202

Dear God,

We are your ambassadors, representing your kingdom in the earth. I pray for My Husband's place of victory because You have already conquered the enemy. When My Husband prays in your name, according to your Word, his requests are good as done. Thank You for giving him authority in your name. In Jesus' name I pray, Amen.

• • •

"For the Lord, your God is going with you! He will fight for you against your enemies, and he will give you victory!"
Deuteronomy 20:4

DAY 203

Dear God,

Thank You for your protective presence. Cover My Husband today. Let your faithful promises be his armor and defense.
In Jesus' name I pray, Amen.

• • •

He will cover you with his feathers. He will shelter you with his wings. His faithful promises are your armor and protection.
Psalm 91:4

PROTECTION

DAY 204

Dear God,

I pray a prophetic upgrading of My Husband's thought life. Today, may My Husband wear the helmet of salvation to protect his mind from negative thoughts. May he be intentional to protect his integrity and righteous to protect his reputation. Give My Husband peace to guide his every step and faith to secure his future. Grant My Husband dominion and authority over his mind to cancel the effect of negative, self-defeating words. In Jesus' name I pray, Amen.

• • •

Get wisdom; develop good judgement.
Proverbs 4:5

DAY 205

Dear God,

Open My Husband's eyes to see his gifts and abilities the way You see them. May he be mindful to reject every limiting belief that the enemy tries to release. Help My Husband conduct his affairs in the most discerning, expeditious, and fiscally wise manner today. Open new doors of opportunity and allow only those with divine assignments to be drawn to him. In Jesus' name I pray, Amen.

• • •

Do not forget my words or turn away from them. Do not turn your back on wisdom, for she will protect you. Love her, and she will guard you. Getting wisdom is the wisest thing you can do! And whatever else you do, develop good judgement.
Proverbs 4:6-7

DAY 206

Dear God,

I pray that My Husband has the mind of Christ. Give him the wisdom and the will to guard his thoughts today. In Jesus' name I pray, Amen.

• • •

Do not copy the behavior and customs of this world, but let God transform you into a new person by changing the way you think. Then you will learn to know God's will for you, which is good and pleasing and perfect.
Romans 12:2

DAY 207

Dear God,

Place a warrior anointing on My Husband so that he may possess the power You have given him. When My Husband feels the weight of the world on his shoulders, I pray that he will not worry, but that he receives your peace which transcends all human understanding. Strengthen the hedge of protection around his life, his possessions, our family, his friends, his heart, and his ministry. In Jesus' name I pray, Amen.

• • •

But thank God! He gives us victory over sin and death through our Lord Jesus Christ.
1 Corinthians 15:57

PROTECTION

DAY 208

Dear God,

I release My Husband's name into the atmosphere and declare that he has a good reputation. I pray that My Husband's name be associated with excellence, integrity, holiness, generosity, vision, health, and faith. No weapon formed against him shall prosper because My Husband is anointed for such a time as this. In Jesus' name I pray, Amen.

• • •

But in that coming day no weapon turned against you will succeed. You will silence every voice raised up to accuse you. These benefits are enjoyed by the servants of the Lord; their vindication will come from me. I, the Lord, have spoken!
Isaiah 54:17

DAY 209

Dear God,

Thank You that we can influence our destiny with your Word. Help My Husband take command and direct the trajectory of his life through prayer and fasting. May he guard his heart diligently to stay on course. In Jesus' name I pray, Amen.

• • •

Guard your heart above all else, for it determines the course of your life.
Proverbs 4:23

DAY 210

Dear God,

I pray that My Husband will be anxious for nothing, but in everything be prayerful and thankful. When making his requests known to You, give My Husband faith to know that You hear and answer his prayers. Guard his heart and his mind in stillness and in the quiet times.
In Jesus' name I pray, Amen.

* * *

Now may the Lord of peace himself give you his peace at all times and in every situation. The Lord be with you all.
2 Thessalonians 3:16

DAY 211

Dear God,

We know that My Husband is here by design and You have equipped him to complete a specific assignment. I speak abundance over My Husband's life as he walks in peace and truth. Thank You that My Husband's blessings will never be hindered, rather they are overflowing.
In Jesus' name I pray, Amen.

• • •

The thief's purpose is to steal and kill and destroy. My purpose is to give a rich and satisfying life.
John 10:10

PROTECTION

Peace

DAY 212

Dear God,

Thank You that My Husband is considerate of me, respectful towards me, and gentle with me. Thank You, Lord, that even though I may be weaker physically, My Husband and I are growing spiritually and are equal heirs of Christ. Let nothing hinder My Husband's prayers.
In Jesus' name I pray, Amen.

• • •

In the same way, you husbands must give honor to your wives. Treat your wife with understanding as you live together. She may be weaker than you are, but she is your equal partner in God's gift of new life. Treat her as you should so your prayers will not be hindered.
1 Peter 3:7

DAY 213

Dear God,

You are a God of order, so remind My Husband to see You early and consult You about ordering his day. Reveal to My Husband the proper order so that he may walk in your blessing and favor. Align every facet of this day with your original plan and purpose for him. In Jesus' name I pray, Amen.

• • •

But be sure that everything is done properly and in order.
1 Corinthians 14:40

PEACE

DAY 214

Dear God,

Fill My Husband's heart with your peace and joy. Remind My Husband to stand firm on your promises so that he can declare them throughout the day. Thank You that My Husband seeks wisdom and understanding in your Word. Help him to continue to follow after You for without You he can do nothing. May your Spirit lead him. In Jesus' name I pray, Amen.

* * *

For all of God's promises have been fulfilled in Christ with a resounding "Yes!" And through Christ, our "Amen" (which means "Yes") ascends to God for his glory.
2 Corinthians 1:20

DAY 215

Dear God,

Your Word says that a heart at peace gives life to the body. Thank You that My Husband has a peaceful heart that ushers in good health. We praise You for all the wonderful ways You provide for My Husband's needs.
In Jesus' name I pray, Amen.

• • •

A peaceful heart leads to a healthy body;
jealousy is like cancer in the bones.
Proverbs 14:30

DAY 216

Dear God,

Let nothing separate My Husband
from You or hinder his prayers.
Make him more like You.
In Jesus' name I pray, Amen.

* * *

For we are God's masterpiece. He has created
us anew in Christ Jesus, so we can do the
good things he planned for us long ago.
Ephesians 2:10

DAY 217

Dear God,

I speak to this day that it will cooperate with your plans for My Husband. Thank You for divine connections that advance your kingdom. Give My Husband wisdom and understanding to be more efficient in his work. Open doors to new opportunities. Bless the work of his hands as he chooses to glorify You. In Jesus' name I pray, Amen.

• • •

"I know all the things you do, and I have opened a door for you that no one can close. You have little strength, yet you obeyed my word and did not deny me."
Revelation 3:8

PEACE

DAY 218

Dear God,

Let My Husband be in sync and in season with your original plan and purpose. Give My Husband prophetic revelation so that his prayers are like strategic missiles that reach their targets and accomplish the divine purpose for which they have been sent. Let your fire fill his heart.
In Jesus' name I pray, Amen.

* * *

> You did not choose me. I chose you. I appointed you to go and produce lasting fruit, so that the Father will give you whatever you ask for, using my name.
> John 15:16

DAY 219

Dear God,

Shape us into a beautiful representation of You. Even though we are far from perfect, we know nothing is too hard for You. Please make My Husband the man You have purposed him to be. Help him to be moldable in your hands. In Jesus' name I pray, Amen.

• • •

Put on your new nature and be renewed as you learn to know your Creator and become like him.
Colossians 3:10

DAY 220

Dear God,

Inspire My Husband to motivate his friends, family, and business partners toward acts of love and good deeds. Prompt My Husband to foster spiritual growth in the lives of others. In Jesus' name I pray, Amen.

• • •

Let us think of ways to motivate one another to acts of love and good works.
Hebrews 10:24

DAY 221

Dear God,

This is a new season and You are aligning My Husband with your original plan and purpose. Let him be perfectly in sync and in season with You. I pray that every element of today will cooperate with what My Husband expects to accomplish. In Jesus' name I pray, Amen.

• • •

Good planning and hard work lead to prosperity, but hasty shortcuts lead to poverty.
Proverbs 21:5

PEACE

DAY 222

Dear God,

Align My Husband's thinking with your thinking, his attitude with your attitude, and his thoughts with your thoughts. Purify his mind to be a reflection of You. In Jesus' name I pray, Amen.

• • •

Instead, let the Spirit renew your thoughts and attitudes. Put on your new nature, created to be like God—truly righteous and holy.
Ephesians 4:23-24

DAY 223

Dear God,

You are My Husband's power source and he will do what it takes to walk out his mission and assignments each and every day. Help My Husband to properly plug into prayer to hear your voice. Keep his mind and heart in agreement with what You are saying about his life and future.
In Jesus' name I pray, Amen.

• • •

We also pray that you will be strengthened with all his glorious power so you will have all the endurance and patience you need. May you be filled with joy.
Colossians 1:11

DAY 224

Dear God,

I decree your will and your Word over
My Husband's life. Give My Husband
a deeper revelation of who he is in
Christ and sharpen his sensitivity
to the authority he has in You.
In Jesus' name I pray, Amen.

• • •

So, we can say with confidence, "The
Lord is my helper, so I will have no fear.
What can mere people do to me?"
Hebrews 13:6

DAY 225

Dear God,

Thank You that My Husband longs to partner with You to advance your kingdom. May My Husband's priority not be to be seen as righteous by men, but to be seen as righteous by You. Create in him a clean heart, Lord, so that he can be trusted with your strategic plans.
In Jesus' name I pray, Amen.

• • •

God blesses those whose hearts are pure, for they will see God.
Matthew 5:8

PEACE

DAY 226

Dear God,

As your child, I pray that My Husband will form partnerships and collaborations with individuals who are believers and accept You. In Jesus' name I pray, Amen.

• • •

Two people are better off than one, for they can help each other succeed. If one person falls, the other can reach out and help. But someone who falls alone is in real trouble.
Ecclesiastes 4:9-10

DAY 227

Dear God,

May all My Husband's desires
and words align with Yours.
In Jesus' name I pray, Amen.

• • •

Anyone who listens to my teaching and
follows it is wise, like a person who builds a
house on solid rock. Though the rain comes
in torrents and the floodwaters rise and the
winds beat against that house, it will not
collapse because it is built on bedrock.
Matthew 7:24-25

DAY 228

Dear God,

Thank You that My Husband chooses to honor You with his thoughts. May he resist negative, self-defeating mindsets and choose instead to speak life and strength into his day. I pray that My Husband is blessed—all his physical needs are met, and that he has more than enough to give to others. Thank You that My Husband works diligently and with a spirit of excellence. And finally, I declare that his home and workspace are peaceful.
In Jesus' name I pray, Amen.

• • •

Take delight in the Lord, and he will give you your heart's desires. Commit everything you do to the Lord. Trust him, and he will help you.
Psalm 37:4-5

DAY 229

Dear God,

We know that our blessings are voice activated. I pray that My Husband prays and declares out loud what You have put on his heart. You desire great things for My Husband, so I pray that he aligns his speech with those great plans. Give him a fresh excitement to serve You. In Jesus' name I pray, Amen.

• • •

May the words of my mouth and the meditation of my heart be pleasing to you, O Lord, my rock, and my redeemer.
Psalm 19:14

PEACE

DAY 230

Dear God,

We believe that You want only the best for us. Thank You for responding to My Husband and showing him your plans. I pray that nothing is impossible for My Husband—
he will succeed and not fail.
In Jesus' name I pray, Amen.

• • •

For the word of God will never fail.
Luke 1:37

DAY 231

Dear God,

You know what is truly in our hearts. Weed out anything that is not like You. Let our words reflect your Word, our hearts reflect your heart, and our thoughts reflect your thoughts. We submit to your complete control. As we renew our mind with your Word, everything is changing for our good and your glory.
In Jesus' name I pray, Amen.

• • •

And we know that God causes everything to work together for the good of those who love God and are called according to his purpose for them.
Romans 8:28

DAY 232

Dear God,

Show My Husband how to make every effort to live in peace with all men. Thank You for guiding him to settle every conflict quickly and peacefully, and for having the courage to do so.
In Jesus' name I pray, Amen.

• • •

Work at living in peace with everyone, and work at living a holy life, for those who are not holy will not see the Lord.
Hebrews 12:14

DAY 233

Dear God,

Thank You that You never forsake those who seek You. Lift any burdens, worry, anxiety, or fret from My Husband's shoulders. Teach him to rest in, lean on, and confidently put his trust in You. In Jesus' name I pray, Amen.

• • •

Fear of the Lord is the foundation of wisdom. Knowledge of the Holy One results in good judgement.
Proverbs 9:10

PEACE

DAY 234

Dear God,

Thank You that prayer is how You prepare us for challenges. Renew our zeal to seek You daily in prayer. Place upon My Husband an anointing for balance so he never crams so much into a day that he leaves no time for You. In Jesus' name I pray, Amen.

* * *

Dear friend, I hope all is well with you and that you are as healthy in body as you are strong in spirit.
3 John 1:2

DAY 235

Dear God,

We will not limit our expectations to what we see in the natural. Our lives are hidden in You. I pray that My Husband receives all that comes with being a child of God. I declare that My Husband's life is blessed. The works of his hands are blessed. Joy, peace, prosperity, success, and influence are his constant companions. Empower My Husband to maintain a kingdom perspective. In Jesus' name I pray, Amen.

•   •   •

O my son, give me your heart. May your eyes take delight in following my ways.
Proverbs 23:26

Peace

DAY 236

Dear God,

We bring our thoughts into divine alignment today. Help My Husband choose to think about things that are true, noble, authentic, and gracious. May he meditate on the best and the beautiful like Jabez. I declare that as My Husband focuses on the positive, new cycles of victory, success, and prosperity will exist in his life.
In Jesus' name I pray, Amen.

• • •

And now, dear brothers and sisters, one final thing. Fix your thoughts on what is true, and honorable, and right, and pure, and lovely, and admirable. Think about things that are excellent and worthy of praise.
Philippians 4:8

DAY 237

Dear God,

Thank You that My Husband walks in the knowledge and authority You have provided. I pray that My Husband possesses his inheritance in You and that nothing threatens his peace and stability.
In Jesus' name I pray, Amen.

• • •

But you are not like that, for you are a chosen people. You are royal priests, a holy nation, God's very own possession. As a result, you can show others the goodness of God, for he called you out of the darkness into his wonderful light.
1 Peter 2:9

PEACE

DAY 238

Dear God,

We know that nothing is too hard for You. Empower My Husband to praise You today when the enemy presents a feeling of worry. Remind My Husband that he can place everything that he cares about on your shoulders. In Jesus' name I pray, Amen.

* * *

Is anything too hard for the Lord? I will return about this time next year, and Sarah will have a son."
Genesis 18:14

DAY 239

Dear God,

Thank You that My Husband does not let circumstances dictate his future. Show him how to walk in peace, how to take authority over his circumstances, and how to decree the will of God into manifestation. In Jesus' name I pray, Amen.

• • •

At that time, you will not need to ask me for anything. I tell you the truth, you will ask the Father directly, and he will grant your request because you use my name.
John 16:23

DAY 240

Dear God,

Make My Husband more like You
and help him to hold nothing
back from You. Let him release
You to work in his life fully.
In Jesus' name I pray, Amen.

• • •

"Keep on asking, and you will receive
what you ask for. Keep on seeking, and
you will find. Keep on knocking, and
the door will be opened to you. For
everyone who asks, receives. Everyone
who seeks, finds. And to everyone who
knocks, the door will be opened.
Matthew 7:7-8

DAY 241

Dear God,

You have given us authority over the enemy. May My Husband walk in that authority today. I declare that the struggle is over. I pray for sudden surprises, supernatural increase, favor, and influence. My Husband is anointed for a new season. Old things are passed away, all things are new. Make My Husband whole and strong—his heart filled with peace, mind focused, and life shining for your glory alone. In Jesus' name I pray, Amen.

• • •

May the Lord richly bless both you and your children. May you be blessed by the Lord, who made heaven and earth.
Psalm 115:14-15

PEACE

Faith

DAY 242

Dear God,

I pray You open My Husband's ears to hear You, and his eyes to see You. Increase his sensitivity and spiritual acuity to detect your voice. May he know at the end of the day that You have spoken to him today.
In Jesus' name I pray, Amen.

* * *

Then he added, "Pay close attention to what you hear. The closer you listen, the more understanding you will be given—and you will receive even more.
Mark 4:24

DAY 243

Dear God,

Show My Husband how to praise his way through today. Allow praise to continually flow from his mouth. I am praying Lord that My Husband stands firm in faith and remember your goodness today. In Jesus' name I pray, Amen.

• • •

> But I will give repeated thanks to the Lord, praising him to everyone.
> Psalm 109:30

DAY 244

Dear God,

Give My Husband the faith to stand firm in the center of your will, fully expecting You to perform miracles, wonders, and mighty acts on his behalf.
In Jesus' name I pray, Amen.

• • •

"You don't have enough faith," Jesus told them. "I tell you the truth, if you had faith even as small as a mustard seed, you could say to this mountain, 'Move from here to there,' and it would move. Nothing would be impossible."
Matthew 17:20

DAY 245

Dear God,

Let whatever My Husband does in both speech and action today - let it be done in the name of Jesus. In Jesus' name I pray, Amen.

• • •

And whatever you do or say, do it as a representative of the Lord Jesus, giving thanks through him to God the Father.
Colossians 3:17

DAY 246

Dear God,

You are moving My Husband toward your perfect plan. Help him to not be moved by circumstances; rather help him to walk by faith. I pray that My Husband keeps on believing until your Will manifests. In Jesus' name I pray, Amen.

• • •

I tell you the truth, you can say to this mountain, 'May you be lifted up and thrown into the sea,' and it will happen. But you must really believe it will happen and have no doubt in your heart.
Mark 11:23

DAY 247

Dear God,

Fill My Husband with the power of the Holy Spirit so that he will not let anyone, or anything prevent him from worshiping You. May he be like Daniel, who refused to hide his faith even though it was punishable by death. No matter what pressures are placed on him, let My Husband always praise and worship You.
In Jesus' name I pray, Amen.

• • •

> Then I will praise God's name with singing, and I will honor him with thanksgiving.
> Psalm 69:30

FAITH

DAY 248

Dear God,

All we need is faith the size of a mustard seed. With that much faith we can tell mountains to move. Strengthen My Husband's belief that You will meet every need and respond to every care. I pray that My Husband brings everything to You knowing that nothing is too small. Increase his faith. Help him to depend completely on You. In Jesus' name I pray, Amen.

• • •

And though you started with little,
you will end with much.
Job 8:7

DAY 249

Dear God,

You said in your Word that all
things are possible; therefore, give
My Husband the faith to believe
that the impossible is possible
in every area of his life and that
he will not be limited by man.
In Jesus' name I pray, Amen.

• • •

"You can pray for anything, and if you
have faith, you will receive it."
Matthew 21:22

DAY 250

Dear God,

Your Word says that your plans are to give us hope and a future. So, we greet today in anticipation of the good things You have prepared for us. Let your wisdom, understanding, and insight be with My Husband today. Cause him to walk in sync with your will for his life. In Jesus' name I pray, Amen.

* * *

I pray that God, the source of hope, will fill you completely with joy and peace because you trust in him. Then you will overflow with confident hope through the power of the Holy Spirit.
Romans 15:13

DAY 251

Dear God,

Assure My Husband that he has nothing to fear because You are his light to guide him and his salvation to sustain him. Help My Husband conquer any fear with the certainty that You are greater than any spiritual or physical enemy. Thank You for being the mighty stronghold in My Husband's life.
In Jesus' name I pray, Amen.

• • •

The Lord is my light and my salvation so why should I be afraid? The Lord is my fortress, protecting me from danger, so why should I tremble?
Psalm 27:1

FAITH

DAY 252

Dear God,

I ask that You open My Husband's mind to understand your Word. May the Holy Spirit be his teacher so that he will be enlightened by Scripture. In Jesus' name I pray, Amen.

• • •

Then he opened their minds to understand the Scriptures.
Luke 24:45

DAY 253

Dear God,

Amidst all things vying for My Husband's attention today, help him to tune his ear to music, messages, and men that will further his faith. Mature his faith as a direct result of what and who he listens to.
In Jesus' name I pray, Amen.

• • •

So, faith comes from hearing, that is, hearing the Good News about Christ.
Romans 10:17

DAY 254

Dear God,

We expect that what we pray shall come to pass once it has been sealed in the Spirit. You have already released your plans for us before the foundations of the earth and have assigned a specific time and season for them to come to pass. Discipline My Husband's mouth so that he speaks only words of faith and releases only your plans and purpose for his life. In Jesus' name I pray, Amen.

* * *

So, he will do to me whatever he has planned. He controls my destiny.
Job 23:14

DAY 255

Dear God,

Make My Husband like a tree planted by streams of living water. When his pay seems slim, when bills increase, or when he just needs to hear from You, I pray he will not feel burdened, anxious, or worried. Instead show My Husband how to sink his roots deep into the living water which never runs dry. In Jesus' name I pray, Amen.

• • •

But blessed are those who trust in the Lord and have made the Lord their hope and confidence. They are like trees planted along a riverbank, with roots that reach deep into the water. Such trees are not bothered by the heat or worried by long months of drought. Their leaves stay green, and they never stop producing fruit.
Jeremiah 17:7-8

FAITH

DAY 256

Dear God,

Teach us to see with our spiritual eyes as readily as we see with our physical eyes. For You are much greater than anything we face here on earth. Help My Husband to dig into the Spirit in prayer so that he is comfortable in your realm and how it functions. Bring his words into alignment with what heaven is saying about him today. Order My Husband's steps in your Word, today. In Jesus' name I pray, Amen.

* * *

For the word of God is alive and powerful. It is sharper than the sharpest two-edged sword, cutting between soul and spirit, between joint and marrow. It exposes our innermost thoughts and desires.
Hebrews 4:12

DAY 257

Dear God,

I pray that your perfect Will be done in and through My Husband today. Let nothing prevent My Husband from walking in the fullness of what You have for him. In Jesus' name I pray, Amen.

• • •

Then he said to the crowd, "If any of you wants to be my follower, you must give up your own way, take up your cross daily, and follow me."
Luke 9:23

DAY 258

Dear God,

Thank You that we have the mind of Christ and therefore see things from above. Give us power and new dimensions of divine revelation. I declare that every mental block is cleared, giving the Holy Spirit unrestricted access to My Husband's mind, soul, and spirit. Father, reveal your assignment and agenda for My Husband today. May he operate in your correct timing. In Jesus' name I pray, Amen.

• • •

"I have told you all this so that you may have peace in me. Here on earth you will have many trials and sorrows. But take heart because I have overcome the world."
John 16:33

DAY 259

Dear God,

Help us to pray your truth, and not the facts. The fact may be that we have bills, but the truth is that You shall supply all our needs according to your riches in glory. Thank You for the truth. Help My Husband to believe your Word over the fact of the situations he faces. As we declare your truth, may My Husband's circumstances change for the best. Thank You, Father, for the victory. In Jesus' name I pray, Amen.

• • •

Faith shows the reality of what
we hope for; it is the evidence
of things we cannot see.
Hebrews 11:1

FAITH

DAY 260

Dear God,

Without You, we can do nothing. I pray that My Husband presses through in prayer for a breakthrough. Help him to pray more, praise more, give more, believe more, and hope more. Bring stability to his emotions and give him a fortified mind that is stable and steadfast in faith.
In Jesus' name I pray, Amen.

* * *

Then the man said, "Let me go, for the dawn is breaking!" But Jacob said, "I will not let you go unless you bless me."
Genesis 32:26

DAY 261

Dear God,

We resolve today that we will not stop praying until You answer. Teach My Husband how to reject words of doubt and disbelief. When the enemy tries to discourage him, remind him that through You everything he needs is available. All My Husband's needs are supplied according to your riches in glory. In Jesus' name I pray, Amen.

• • •

And we are confident that he hears us whenever we ask for anything that pleases him.
1 John 5:14

DAY 262

Dear God,

As your child, I pray that My Husband
will lead unbelievers to accept
You as their Lord and Savior.
In Jesus' name I pray, Amen.

• • •

When you produce much fruit, you are my true
disciples. This brings great glory to my Father.
John 15:8

DAY 263

Dear God,

Put your Word in My Husband's mouth so that when he speaks, your plans and purposes are aligned.
In Jesus' name I pray, Amen.

• • •

The crowd was listening to everything Jesus said. And because he was nearing Jerusalem, he told them a story to correct the impression that the Kingdom of God would begin right away.
Luke 19:11

FAITH

DAY 264

Dear God,

You put the power of life and death within our tongues. So, I speak life over My Husband's day. Let your wisdom, understanding, and prophetic insight be upon My Husband today. Open his ears and grant him the ability to hear clearly as You give creative ideas to be more fruitful and productive. In Jesus' name I pray, Amen.

• • •

Then the way you live will always honor and please the Lord, and your lives will produce every kind of good fruit. All the while, you will grow as you learn to know God better and better.
Colossians 1:10

DAY 265

Dear God,

Tune My Husband's spiritual ears to the frequency of your voice. I pray he will be open to the various ways You can and do speak to him. Whether dreaming at night, driving in his car, waiting for a client, or sitting at his desk, I pray My Husband will be spiritually sensitive to your still voice speaking to his inner man. In Jesus' name I pray, Amen.

• • •

For God speaks again and again, though people do not recognize it. He speaks in dreams, in visions of the night, when deep sleep falls on people as they lie in their beds.
Job 33:14-15

DAY 266

Dear God,

Let every gift and calling You have
deposited within My Husband
be released in its perfect time.
In Jesus' name I pray, Amen.

• • •

They are like trees planted along the riverbank,
bearing fruit each season. Their leaves never
wither, and they prosper in all they do.
Psalm 1:3

DAY 267

Dear God,

Without faith, it is impossible to please You. I pray that My Husband throws full conviction into his words so that heaven and earth will align to answer his prayers. Show My Husband how to make deliberate and conscious decisions to agree with You. In Jesus' name I pray, Amen.

• • •

> Watch out that you do not lose what we have worked so hard to achieve. Be diligent so that you receive your full reward.
> 2 John 1:8

FAITH

DAY 268

Dear God,

There is no question that Jesus was always 'prayed up'. I pray that My Husband stays connected to You and that he values his prayer time with You. Then, when My Husband is faced with a situation, he will know just what to do.
In Jesus' name I pray, Amen.

• • •

But Jesus often withdrew to
the wilderness for prayer.
Luke 5:16

DAY 269

Dear God,

There is no doubt in my mind that You want to bless and prosper My Husband. Thank You that My Husband is rewarded for diligently seeking You. I pray that his unshakable faith pleases You. In Jesus' name I pray, Amen.

* * *

And it is impossible to please God without faith. Anyone who wants to come to him must believe that God exists and that he rewards those who sincerely seek him.
Hebrews 11:6

DAY 270

Dear God,

We know that through our positive confessions of faith, we can influence how the world around us takes form. Thank You for prayer—the opportunity to speak the language of change. As My Husband prays, may the faith invested in his words affect anything and everything that is in his path. I cancel the effect of negative, self-defeating thoughts. Give My Husband a fresh mind and fresh excitement—an anticipation of the good things You will do today. In Jesus' name I pray, Amen.

• • •

Confess your sins to each other and pray for each other so that you may be healed. The earnest prayer of a righteous person has great power and produces wonderful results.
James 5:16

DAY 271

Dear God,

With faith the size of a mustard seed, we can tell mountains to move. I stand in faith today, believing that You will meet every one of My Husband's needs and respond to his every care. May My Husband's faith rise today as he depends completely on You. In Jesus' name I pray, Amen.

• • •

God is not a man, so he does not lie. He is not human, so he does not change his mind. Has he ever spoken and failed to act? Has he ever promised and not carried it through?
Numbers 23:19

FAITH

Love

DAY 272

Dear God,

I pray that My Husband continues
to keep his desire to please
You, serve You, and love You
at the forefront of his life.
In Jesus' name I pray, Amen.

• • •

Obviously, I am not trying to win the approval
of people, but of God. If pleasing people
were my goal, I would not be Christ's servant.
Galatians 1:10

DAY 273

Dear God,

Remind My Husband that he can draw near to You with a sincere heart in full assurance of faith. Help him to approach the throne with confidence and when he is weak or doubtful, remind him that he has been restored by You. In Jesus' name I pray, Amen.

• • •

So, let us come boldly to the throne of our gracious God. There we will receive his mercy, and we will find grace to help us when we need it most.
Hebrews 4:16

LOVE

DAY 274

Dear God,

Give My Husband a discerning spirit and intuitive heart. Help him to foster godly character and friendships, and to know that You will never lead him astray. In Jesus' name I pray, Amen.

• • •

The godly give good advice to their friends; the wicked lead them astray.
Proverbs 12:26

DAY 275

Dear God,

Remind My Husband repeatedly
of your great love for him today.
In Jesus' name I pray, Amen.

• • •

Yet I still dare to hope when I remember this:
The faithful love of the Lord never ends. His
mercies never cease. Great is his faithfulness;
his mercies begin afresh each morning.
Lamentations 3:21-23

DAY 276

Dear God,

Stir My Husband to love You with all his mind. Keep him from developing religious routine; Show him how to have an intimate relationship with You. Let his mind be centered on You, focused on You, and set on You. In Jesus' name I pray, Amen.

• • •

Jesus replied, "'You must love the Lord your God with all your heart, all your soul, and all your mind.'
Matthew 22:37

DAY 277

Dear God,

We know that You can do anything—far more than we could ever imagine or request. You work beyond My Husband's wildest dreams and imagination. So, open his mind and heart to the supernatural. In Jesus' name I pray, Amen.

• • •

Now all glory to God, who is able, through his mighty power at work within us, to accomplish infinitely more than we might ask or think.
Ephesians 3:20

LOVE

DAY 278

Dear God,

Your Word says that a friend loves at all times. Teach My Husband what it means to be a friend who always loves, especially when a friend is hard to love. And Lord, bless him with a friend who will do the same. In Jesus' name I pray, Amen.

• • •

When Job prayed for his friends, the Lord restored his fortunes. In fact, the Lord gave him twice as much as before!
Job 42:10

DAY 279

Dear God,

May My Husband pause often to
praise You for who You are and
thank You for what You do.
In Jesus' name I pray, Amen.

* * *

Shout with joy to the Lord, all the earth!
Worship the Lord with gladness. Come
before him, singing with joy. Acknowledge
that the Lord is God! He made us, and we
are his. We are his people, the sheep of his
pasture. Enter his gates with thanksgiving; go
into his courts with praise. Give thanks to him
and praise his name. For the Lord is good.
His unfailing love continues forever, and his
faithfulness continues to each generation.
Psalm 100:1-5

DAY 280

Dear God,

Release every resource that we need to fulfill our assignment. Your Word says that You ordained praise to silence the enemy. So, let My Husband worship You every minute of every day of the week; let his worship be a lifestyle that touches the world. In Jesus' name I pray, Amen.

* * *

That is why I can never stop praising you; I declare your glory all day long.
Psalm 71:8

DAY 281

Dear God,

Thank You for truly caring for us. I pray that My Husband never doubts your love for him. You are his source of wisdom. You are the one who renews his strength. It is your desire that My Husband prospers and be in good health. In Jesus' name I pray, Amen.

• • •

"For I know the plans I have for you," says the Lord. "They are plans for good and not for disaster, to give you a future and a hope."
Jeremiah 29:11

DAY 282

Dear God,

Help My Husband to run to You because You are more than able to accomplish everything that concerns him today.
In Jesus' name I pray, Amen.

• • •

Give all your worries and cares to God, for he cares about you.
1 Peter 5:7

DAY 283

Dear God,

Teach My Husband how to speak the truth in love. If he must confront a business colleague, a friend, family, or even me, prompt him to apply mercy and grace before he speaks. In Jesus' name I pray, Amen.

• • •

Instead, we will speak the truth in love, growing in every way more and more like Christ, who is the head of his body, the church.
Ephesians 4:15

DAY 284

Dear God,

Thank You that My Husband walks in love as your Word instructs him to. Help him also to walk in proactive forgiveness and to cherish his relationships over things—over his accomplishments, goals, tasks, and even himself. That is the richest life possible because with your love he will not fail.
In Jesus' name I pray, Amen.

• • •

Love is patient and kind. Love is not jealous or boastful or proud or rude. It does not demand its own way. It is not irritable, and it keeps no record of being wronged. It does not rejoice about injustice but rejoices whenever the truth wins out. Love never gives up, never loses faith, is always hopeful, and endures through every circumstance. Prophecy and speaking in unknown languages and special knowledge will become useless. But love will last forever!
1 Corinthians 13:4-7

DAY 285

Dear God,

Stretch how My Husband begins to trust You for and what He will accomplish in You. Renew My Husband's faith. Rejuvenate his love for You as he steps further into the life You have given him since he first gave his heart to You.
In Jesus' name I pray, Amen.

* * *

Those who know your name trust in you, for you, O Lord, do not abandon those who search for you.
Psalm 9:10

DAY 286

Dear God,

Help My Husband treat others the way he would like to be treated—with love, honor, and respect. In Jesus' name I pray, Amen.

* * *

Do to others whatever you would like them to do to you. This is the essence of all that is taught in the law and the prophets.
Matthew 7:12

DAY 287

Dear God,

You are the only great and awesome God. Sharpen our awareness of your presence and power. Let My Husband know and experience your love in a deeper way, so he will not give in to fear. Help My Husband to not be afraid to follow your instructions because nothing he will face today, or any day is bigger than You.
In Jesus' name I pray, Amen.

• • •

I prayed to the Lord, and he answered me. He freed me from all my fears.
Psalm 34:4

DAY 288

Dear God,

Thank You for giving us the power to transform the world around us. Move My Husband into greatness and empower him to hold nothing back. May he pray to change circumstances and to change the hearts and minds of future generations. In Jesus' name I pray, Amen.

* * *

Jesus looked at them intently and said, "Humanly speaking, it is impossible. But with God everything is possible."
Matthew 19:26

DAY 289

Dear God,

Please bless My Husband with
a cheerful, and positive heart—a
heart that nourishes his body and
soul according to your Word.
In Jesus' name I pray, Amen.

• • •

*If you look for me wholeheartedly,
you will find me.
Jeremiah 29:13*

LOVE

DAY 290

Dear God,

Thank You for giving My Husband an overriding sense of peace, love, mercy, favor, and the absolute assurance that You are in control. In Jesus' name I pray, Amen.

• • •

Even when I walk through the darkest valley, I will not be afraid, for you are close beside me. Your rod and your staff protect and comfort me.
Psalm 23:4

DAY 291

Dear God,

I pray that My Husband's love for You will abound more and more each day. May he seek You first for knowledge and depth of insight. Give him discernment to make the best choices.
In Jesus' name I pray, Amen.

• • •

I pray that your love will overflow more and more, and that you will keep on growing in knowledge and understanding. For I want you to understand what really matters, so that you may live pure and blameless lives until the day of Christ's return.
Philippians 1:9-10

DAY 292

Dear God,

Thank You for equipping My Husband with unique gifts and talents. Continue to show him how to use his gifts to proclaim your kingdom and to showcase your love. In Jesus' name I pray, Amen.

• • •

In his grace, God has given us different gifts for doing certain things well. So, if God has given you the ability to prophesy, speak out with as much faith as God has given you. If your gift is serving others, serve them well. If you are a teacher, teach well. If your gift is to encourage others, be encouraging. If it is giving, give generously. If God has given you leadership ability, take the responsibility seriously. And if you have a gift for showing kindness to others, do it gladly.
Romans 12:6-8

DAY 293

Dear God,

All that we have belongs to You. Thank You that My Husband is a good steward of all that You have given him. Give him wisdom to handle money wisely and to make good decisions on how he spends. May My Husband always be paid well for the work that he does. Multiply his riches so that he has more than enough. In Jesus' name I pray, Amen.

• • •

Honor the Lord with your wealth and with the best part of everything you produce. Then he will fill your barns with grain, and your vats will overflow with good wine.
Proverbs 3:9-10

LOVE

DAY 294

Dear God,

Thank You for bringing together everything You have purposed for My Husband.
In Jesus' name I pray, Amen.

• • •

He was the one who prayed to the God of Israel, "Oh, that you would bless me and expand my territory! Please be with me in all that I do and keep me from all trouble and pain!" And God granted him his request.
1 Chronicles 4:10

DAY 295

Dear God,

Give My Husband wisdom in choosing his best friends. While My Husband is called, bring him godly men with whom he can form strong bonds—men who will influence him to follow You more closely, love You more deeply, and listen to You more carefully. In Jesus' name I pray, Amen.

* * *

The godly give good advice to their friends; the wicked lead them astray.
Proverbs 12:26

DAY 296

Dear God,

Help My Husband to not be moved by circumstances, but to walk by faith. Thank You that as My Husband walks according to the Spirit, he bears the fruit of the Spirit—love, joy, peace, gentleness, goodness, temperance, and faith. In Jesus' name I pray, Amen.

• • •

Above all, clothe yourselves with love, which binds us all together in perfect harmony.
Colossians 3:14

DAY 297

Dear God,

I know that what My Husband treasures in his heart is where he will spend his time, resources, and energy. I pray he will fill his heart with the most perfect treasure found in a loving relationship with You. In Jesus' name I pray, Amen.

• • •

Wherever your treasure is, there the desires of your heart will also be.
Matthew 6:21

LOVE

DAY 298

Dear God,

We desire to honor You with our words. Let My Husband's speech always be graceful. May he bless and forgive others so that he is also blessed and forgiven.
In Jesus' name I pray, Amen.

• • •

Bless those who persecute you. Do not curse them; pray that God will bless them.
Romans 12:14

DAY 299

Dear God,

Help us to put your plan into action because we know that if You are for us, then nothing and no one can be against us. I pray that My Husband fills the atmosphere with praise and worship today to prepare for your power and provision. Thank You that My Husband is already victorious in You. In Jesus' name I pray, Amen.

• • •

"The Lord himself will fight for you. Just stay calm."
Exodus 14:14

DAY 300

Dear God,

I pray the meditations of My Husband's heart are pleasing in your sight. Thank You that the wellspring of his heart is pure, so that what flows from it is honorable, reputable, and upright.
In Jesus' name I pray, Amen.

• • •

May the words of my mouth and the meditation of my heart be pleasing to you, O Lord, my rock, and my redeemer.
Psalm 19:14

DAY 301

Dear God,

Let your praise continually be in our mouth. I pray that My Husband always remembers your goodness. In Jesus' name I pray, Amen.

• • •

O Lord, I will honor and praise your name, for you are my God. You do such wonderful things! You planned them long ago, and now you have accomplished them.
Isaiah 25:1

LOVE

Restoration

DAY 302

Dear God,

Increase My Husband's sensitivity to your still small voice speaking to his inner man. May he listen intently, carefully, and attentively to all You have to say.
In Jesus' name I pray, Amen.

* * *

"But all who listen to me will live in peace, untroubled by fear of harm."
Proverbs 1:33

DAY 303

Dear God,

We praise You because we are fearfully and wonderfully made. Keep My Husband's prayer life vibrant and exciting so that he can release everything that is assigned to him. And make this a productive day for My Husband with new strategies and fresh wisdom. In Jesus' name I pray, Amen.

• • •

"And so, my children, listen to me, for all who follow my ways are joyful. Listen to my instruction and be wise. Don't ignore it."
Proverbs 8:32-33

RESTORATION

DAY 304

Dear God,

Help us to develop our senses in the Spirit and our senses for spiritual things. I pray that My Husband develops a prayer life that is active, unrelenting, and thriving. Help him to discipline himself in the ways of the kingdom of God so that he will see good fruit established in his life. In Jesus' name I pray, Amen.

• • •

And the Holy Spirit helps us in our weakness. For example, we do not know what God wants us to pray for. But the Holy Spirit prays for us with groanings that cannot be expressed in words.
Romans 8:26

DAY 305

Dear God,

Put a hunger in My Husband's heart to read, study, and meditate on your Word. Hide your Word in his heart—let it sink into the core of his being. In Jesus' name I pray, Amen.

• • •

I have hidden your word in my heart, that I might not sin against you.
Psalm 119:11

DAY 306

Dear God,

Your Will is our assignment, so we will seek You first and everything needed to fulfill your purposes will be added. Prepare My Husband for the race You have called him to. Strip away his weaknesses. Lighten his load and strengthen him with your love and grace throughout the day. In Jesus' name I pray, Amen.

• • •

Praise the Lord, who is my rock. He trains my hands for war and gives my fingers skill for battle.
Psalm 144:1

DAY 307

Dear God,

We are known as children of God because we bear your fruit. Thank You for your gifts and equipping My Husband to accomplish and achieve the impossible. May he take time to talk with You, listen to your voice, and heed your instructions. Help My Husband to always steward with excellence the blessings You give him.
In Jesus' name I pray, Amen.

• • •

God has given each of you a gift from his great variety of spiritual gifts. Use them well to serve one another.
1 Peter 4:10

RESTORATION

DAY 308

Dear God,

We expect a harvest in your perfect time. Help My Husband to expect the seeds You have planted in him to grow. Remind My Husband that nothing will stop him from reaching the destiny You have planned for him—your purposes will always prevail. In Jesus' name I pray, Amen.

* * *

It is the same with my word. I send it out, and it always produces fruit. It will accomplish all I want it to, and it will prosper everywhere I send it.
Isaiah 55:11

DAY 309

Dear God,

After My Husband has prayed, let him go and be a part of the manifestation of the Word You have given him. Help him to live as an answer to prayer. Release anointing in My Husband's life so that he will accomplish everything that You have planned for him today.
In Jesus' name I pray, Amen.

* * *

"I knew you before I formed you in your mother's womb. Before you were born, I set you apart and appointed you as my prophet to the nations."
Jeremiah 1:5

DAY 310

Dear God,

My Husband has everything he needs in this season to bring forth kingdom strategies and to fulfill divinely ordained assignments. I speak success, prosperity, health, wealth, vision, direction, creativity, holiness, peace, joy, and righteousness from your Spirit to My Husband's spirit today. In Jesus' name I pray, Amen.

• • •

By his divine power, God has given us everything we need for living a godly life. We have received all of this by coming to know him, the one who called us to himself by means of his marvelous glory and excellence.
2 Peter 1:3

DAY 311

Dear God,

When My Husband begins to feel the weight of daily burdens, I pray he will not be discouraged. Help him to praise You when he begins to feel worried. Remind My Husband that You are the burden-bearer and he can put all his hope in You! In Jesus' name I pray, Amen.

* * *

This is my command—be strong and courageous! Do not be afraid or discouraged. For the Lord, your God is with you wherever you go."
Joshua 1:9

DAY 312

Dear God,

Thank You that My Husband is purpose driven, kingdom principled, and success-oriented. Help him to work according to your agenda and to refuse to be distracted by insignificant things. Give My Husband everything he needs to fulfill his assignment during this season. And let today to be loaded with the exact benefits he needs to accomplish his dreams and goals. In Jesus' name I pray, Amen.

• • •

Look straight ahead and fix your eyes on what lies before you. Mark out a straight path for your feet; stay on the safe path. Do not get sidetracked; keep your feet from following evil.
Proverbs 4:25-27

DAY 313

Dear God,

Thank You for filling My Husband with a newness of purpose today. We do not take today for granted because we are asking for a new cycle of power and victory to begin in My Husband's life. Download a fresh vision and purpose in My Husband's spirit so that he may take advantage of every opportunity You bring his way. Remove the cares from yesterday and any worry of tomorrow. In Jesus' name I pray, Amen.

* * *

I am saying this for your benefit, not to place restrictions on you. I want you to do whatever will help you serve the Lord best, with as few distractions as possible.
1 Corinthians 7:35

DAY 314

Dear God,

I pray for My Husband as You have counted him worthy of his calling. I speak to the spiritual, economic, social, and political climate around My Husband and declare that it is now suitable for his ministry, his work, and his ideas to thrive. I establish a supernatural environment for miracles to occur. Wherever My Husband is, change happens. In Jesus' name I pray, Amen.

• • •

So, we keep on praying for you, asking our God to enable you to live a life worthy of his call. May he give you the power to accomplish all the good things your faith prompts you to do.
2 Thessalonians 1:11

DAY 315

Dear God,

Help My Husband to pray through every circumstance until there is a breakthrough. You are making him strong and bold for your kingdom. In Jesus' name I pray, Amen.

• • •

"And so I tell you, keep on asking, and you will receive what you ask for. Keep on seeking, and you will find. Keep on knocking, and the door will be opened to you."
Luke 11:9

RESTORATION

DAY 316

Dear God,

Release every miracle, every
blessing, and every opportunity
You have for My Husband.
In Jesus' name I pray, Amen.

• • •

And God will generously provide all you need.
Then you will always have everything you
need, and plenty left over to share with others.
2 Corinthians 9:8

DAY 317

Dear God,

May You make My Husband whole and put together—in spirit, soul, and body. I declare that My Husband will not just be about 'something'; let him be receptive to doing only 'your thing'.
In Jesus' name I pray, Amen.

• • •

God will make this happen, for he who calls you is faithful.
1 Thessalonians 5:24

DAY 318

Dear God,

Show My Husband how to speak
about You in such a way that
others will want to know more.
In Jesus' name I pray, Amen.

* * *

For I will give you the right words and such
wisdom that none of your opponents
will be able to reply or refute you!
Luke 21:15

DAY 319

Dear God,

I pray that My Husband's spirit is open to the new opportunities and new and pleasant places You are bringing him to in this season. Show My Husband how to speak and think in new ways You direct him to think. He will succeed in this new territory. Thank You for counting My Husband worthy to be relocated to this new place. Thank You for allowing him to grow and mature into the new creation You designed him to be. In Jesus' name I pray, Amen.

• • •

When I was a child, I spoke and thought and reasoned as a child. But when I grew up, I put away childish things.
1 Corinthians 13:11

RESTORATION

DAY 320

Dear God,

We thank You for new and better possibilities. I pray that every element of this day and this year cooperate with your destiny for My Husband. May he greet this year with great anticipation of the good things You have prepared for him. In Jesus' name I pray, Amen.

* * *

May he grant your heart's desires
and make all your plans succeed.
Psalm 20:4

DAY 321

Dear God,

Thank You for equipping My Husband to overcome every obstacle. You have made My Husband in your image and he will create, innovate, strategize, and succeed. Move in his life, his future, and his focus. In Jesus' name I pray, Amen.

• • •

Do not copy the behavior and customs of this world, but let God transform you into a new person by changing the way you think. Then you will learn to know God's will for you, which is good and pleasing and perfect.
Romans 12:2

DAY 322

Dear God,

Give My Husband new strategies for dealing with the challenges he faces. Help him to keep his eyes on You. As his prayers become more specific, give him insight. Direct his mouth to speak life into his circumstances, his day, and his future. Renew his mind with the water of your Word. In Jesus' name I pray, Amen.

* * *

The Lord is close to all who call on him,
yes, to all who call on him in truth.
Psalm 145:18

DAY 323

Dear God,

Renew My Husband's mind today. Transform My Husband's thoughts so that his speech is in perfect alignment with what your Word says he can do and be. In Jesus' name I pray, Amen.

• • •

For we are God's masterpiece. He has created us anew in Christ Jesus, so we can do the good things he planned for us long ago.
Ephesians 2:10

RESTORATION

DAY 324

Dear God,

I pray that You will give My Husband a sound mind today. Help him to have clear, concise, and controlled thinking. Protect him from any spirit of confusion that would attempt to cloud his thinking or jumble his thoughts. In Jesus' name I pray, Amen.

* * *

And the Spirit of the Lord will rest on him—
the Spirit of wisdom and understanding,
the Spirit of counsel and might, the Spirit
of knowledge and the fear of the Lord.
Isaiah 11:2

DAY 325

Dear God,

You have sculpted My Husband and he is well prepared to accomplish every task that awaits him today. Lord, give My Husband creativity, ingenuity, wisdom, a strong work ethic, and a disciplined mind. I pray that You enlarge My Husband's territory and that everything is changing for the best.
In Jesus' name I pray, Amen.

• • •

But there is a spirit within people, the breath of the Almighty within them, that makes them intelligent.
Job 32:8

DAY 326

Dear God,

Open our spiritual eyes and ears to your knowledge. As My Husband desires greater discernment, open his ears to hear your witty ideas and creative inventions. Cause him to see new tactics and strategies that allow him to blaze new trails in his field. And as My Husband advances into new realms spiritually, professionally, and socially, remove all his pride. Direct My Husband to pursue only what You desire for him.
In Jesus' name I pray, Amen.

• • •

Pride leads to disgrace, but with humility comes wisdom.
Proverbs 11:2

DAY 327

Dear God,

Direct My Husband's speech and thoughts to reflect your perfect will for him. We put no limits on what You can do. Thank You for shifting My Husband into new emotional, intellectual, professional, spiritual, and financial territory. In Jesus' name I pray, Amen.

• • •

But those who trust in the Lord will find new strength. They will soar high on wings like eagles. They will run and not grow weary. They will walk and not faint.
Isaiah 40:31

RESTORATION

DAY 328

Dear God,

We know that small thinking limits our achievements. Empower My Husband to cultivate 'possibility thinking'. My Husband is made in your image and after your likeness. May he do things that have never been done before because You know no limits.
In Jesus' name I pray, Amen.

• • •

For the Lord God is our sun and our shield. He gives us grace and glory. The Lord will withhold no good thing from those who do what is right.
Psalm 84:11

DAY 329

Dear God,

I declare that My Husband is a pioneer of new territories. He walks in favor with You and with man. I pray that My Husband will possess all that You are prepared to give and that there will be no holdups, no setbacks, or delays. In Jesus' name I pray, Amen.

• • •

For you know that when your faith is tested, your endurance has a chance to grow.
James 1:3

DAY 330

Dear God,

We reaffirm our commitment to take the limits off You. Allow My Husband to step into your creative mind and do what other people cannot do. Reveal your plans to him so that he can walk unchartered territory. I pray for Moses' anointing to be placed on My Husband so that he is a trailblazer and leader. Enlarge the capacity of his mind. In Jesus' name I pray, Amen.

• • •

For whoever finds me finds life and receives favor from the Lord.
Proverbs 8:35

DAY 331

Dear God,

We know that when My Husband asks something according to your will, You hear him. Empower My Husband to extract wisdom from your Word. Let it shape his thoughts and actions so that he walks in step with You. In Jesus' name I pray, Amen.

• • •

For all of God's promises have been fulfilled in Christ with a resounding "Yes!" And through Christ, our "Amen" (which means "Yes") ascends to God for his glory.
2 Corinthians 1:20

RESTORATION

Trust

DAY 332

Dear God,

I pray that My Husband will always stand for truth. Stir up a desire in him to please You above all else. In Jesus' name I pray, Amen.

* * *

For we speak as messengers approved by God to be entrusted with the Good News. Our purpose is to please God, not people. He alone examines the motives of our hearts.
1 Thessalonians 2:4

DAY 333

Dear God,

We know that we are more than conquerors through You. We also know that when we speak your Word, change happens. So, I stand in faith declaring that all your promises for My Husband are 'yes and amen'. You are more than able to accomplish all that concerns him today. Help My Husband to speak with conviction and to live with complete expectation. In Jesus' name I pray, Amen.

• • •

But when you ask him, be sure that your faith is in God alone. Do not waver, for a person with divided loyalty is as unsettled as a wave of the sea that is blown and tossed by the wind.
James 1:6

TRUST

DAY 334

Dear God,

Enlarge our territory! I know that You are getting ready to blow My Husband's mind with blessings. I pray that all delays, setbacks, and hold ups are destroyed in the name of Jesus. Help My Husband to develop the habit of prayer-walking as You have positioned him for supernatural abundance and favor. In Jesus' name I pray, Amen.

• • •

He was the one who prayed to the God of Israel, "Oh, that you would bless me and expand my territory! Please be with me in all that I do and keep me from all trouble and pain!" And God granted him his request.
1 Chronicles 4:10

DAY 335

Dear God,

Renew, refresh, and reenergize My Husband's mind, body, and soul. In Jesus' name I pray, Amen.

. . .

For God is working in you, giving you the desire and the power to do what pleases him.
Philippians 2:13

DAY 336

Dear God,

Open My Husband's ears to listen
to wise advice and instruction.
Make his inner man sensitive to
the prompts of your still voice.
In Jesus' name I pray, Amen.

* * *

Fools think their own way is right,
but the wise listen to others.
Proverbs 12:15

DAY 337

Dear God,

Teach My Husband to trust in You with all his heart and not lean on his own understanding. Keep him from depending on his own reasoning and to rely on your direction. May My Husband acknowledge You in every decision he has to make today, taking great care to please You and glorify You in all that he does. Remove any confusion that could cloud his thinking and lift any fog that makes your way difficult to see. In Jesus' name I pray, Amen.

• • •

Trust in the Lord with all your heart; do not depend on your own understanding. Seek his will in all you do, and he will show you which path to take.
Proverbs 3:5,6

TRUST

DAY 338

Dear God,

We stand on the promise that everything that pertains to our lives will be released in the correct time and season. Today, I declare new cycles of victory, success, and prosperity in My Husband's life.
In Jesus' name I pray, Amen.

• • •

Always pray in the Spirit and on every occasion. Stay alert and be persistent in your prayers for all believers everywhere.
Ephesians 6:18

DAY 339

Dear God,

When My Husband feels the pressure, stress, and strain of life bearing down on him, remind him to trust in You. May he remember that your commands are not to make life harder, but to make life easier. Help My Husband find joy in your commands that instruct him on how to live life to the fullest. In Jesus' name I pray, Amen.

• • •

This is what I told them: 'Obey me, and I will be your God, and you will be my people. Do everything as I say, and all will be well!'
Jeremiah 7:23

DAY 340

Dear God,

Protect My Husband from being worried or afraid of the future and teach him how to rest in knowing that You have everything under control. Assure My Husband that You can handle every difficulty that comes his way. May he be wise to pray in accordance with your Word and not rely on his own strength or understanding. In Jesus' name I pray, Amen.

• • •

Do not worry about anything; instead, pray about everything. Tell God what you need and thank him for all he has done. Then you will experience God's peace, which exceeds anything we can understand. His peace will guard your hearts and minds as you live in Christ Jesus.
Philippians 4:6-7

DAY 341

Dear God,

Help My Husband to lean into You today for the answers he seeks. May he wait patiently for your timing and trust You to fulfill your promises in whatever manner You see fit. In Jesus' name I pray, Amen.

. . .

Remember the things I have done in the past. For I alone am God! I am God, and there is none like me. Only I can tell you the future before it even happens. Everything I plan will come to pass, for I do whatever I wish.
Isaiah 46:9-10

TRUST

DAY 342

Dear God,

May My Husband refuse the enemy's offers of quick power, easy success, or plentiful possessions. Help him to shut out those lies and to overcome them by listening only to your Truth. In Jesus' name I pray, Amen.

• • •

"Get out of here, Satan," Jesus told him. "For the Scriptures say, 'You must worship the Lord your God and serve only him.'"
Matthew 4:10

DAY 343

Dear God,

Keep My Husband alert, confident, and always prepared to honor You. In Jesus' name I pray, Amen.

• • •

O Lord, I will honor and praise your name, for you are my God. You do such wonderful things! You planned them long ago, and now you have accomplished them.
Isaiah 25:1

DAY 344

Dear God,

We trust You with our whole hearts, so help us not to be wishy-washy. Let what My Husband prays about also be what he speaks in faith. We reject all forms of doublemindedness; it will not find a place in his life. Show My Husband how to command his surroundings in the power of God. May he be steadfast in prayer and faith like Daniel. In Jesus' name I pray, Amen.

• • •

Let us hold tightly without wavering to the hope we affirm, for God can be trusted to keep his promise.
Hebrews 10:23

DAY 345

Dear God,

As My Husband lays his requests and petitions before You each morning, open his spiritual ears to listen for your response in eager expectation. Assure him that You will speak to him and teach him how to recognize your voice.
In Jesus' name I pray, Amen.

• • •

Listen to my voice in the morning, Lord.
Each morning I bring my requests
to you and wait expectantly.
Psalm 5:3

TRUST

DAY 346

Dear God,

Thank You that My Husband is a man of integrity, moral character, honesty, and truth. In Jesus' name I pray, Amen.

• • •

People with integrity walk safely, but those who follow crooked paths will be exposed.
Proverbs 10:9

DAY 347

Dear God,

All that we have belongs to You. Thank You that My Husband is a good steward of all that You have given him. Give him wisdom to handle money wisely and to make good decisions on how he spends. May My Husband always be paid well for the work that he does. Multiply his riches so that he has more than enough.
In Jesus' name I pray, Amen.

• • •

Seek the Kingdom of God above all else,
and he will give you everything you need.
Luke 12:31

DAY 348

Dear God,

We trust You to open unlimited doors of opportunity. I pray that when My Husband is presented with new challenges that he faces them with absolute confidence knowing You are with him. Make any rough place smooth so that he will be even more aware of your presence in his life today. In Jesus' name I pray, Amen.

• • •

Those who trust their own insight are foolish, but anyone who walks in wisdom is safe.
Proverbs 28:26

DAY 349

Dear God,

My Husband is Yours and is led by your hand. Thank You for sending only your best to My Husband as he chooses to walk by faith and not by sight. Grant him the highest of success and prosperity according your plan and purpose.
In Jesus' name I pray, Amen.

• • •

So, let us not get tired of doing what is good. At just the right time we will reap a harvest of blessing if we do not give up.
Galatians 6:9

TRUST

DAY 350

Dear God,

You are up to something good. You have plans for My Husband that are exceedingly abundantly above anything he could ask You for or think of. Thank You for having such a good plan for My Husband.
In Jesus' name I pray, Amen.

• • •

You can make many plans, but the
Lord's purpose will prevail.
Proverbs 19:21

DAY 351

Dear God,

Our own limited thinking can hold us captive. Like Jabez, I boldly ask that You enlarge my Husband's mental capacity. Give him greater capacity to conceive what he must accomplish on your behalf.
In Jesus' name I pray, Amen.

• • •

He was the one who prayed to the God of Israel, "Oh, that you would bless me and expand my territory! Please be with me in all that I do and keep me from all trouble and pain!" And God granted him his request.
1 Chronicles 4:10

DAY 352

Dear God,

Open My Husband's eyes to see how You are working in his life and providing for his needs. Thank You for the streams You have placed in his desert. I pray that My Husband lives in watchful expectation for your new and exciting plans.
In Jesus' name I pray, Amen.

• • •

For I am about to do something new. See, I have already begun! Do you not see it? I will make a pathway through the wilderness. I will create rivers in the dry wasteland.
Isaiah 43:19

DAY 353

Dear God,

I pray that My Husband trusts that You know exactly what he needs. May his relationship with You be his number-one priority. Lead My Husband to seek You and your kingdom first and foremost, knowing everything else will fall into place. In Jesus' name I pray, Amen.

• • •

Seek the Kingdom of God above all else, and he will give you everything you need.
Luke 12:31

TRUST

DAY 354

Dear God,

You made My Husband and You know My Husband. You know his innermost thoughts. You know the desires of his heart and You put capabilities within him. I pray that My Husband runs to You for guidance and that he puts his trust solely in You.
In Jesus' name I pray, Amen.

• • •

Search me, O God, and know my heart; test me and know my anxious thoughts. Point out anything in me that offends you and lead me along the path of everlasting life.
Psalm 139:23-24

DAY 355

Dear God,

I pray that My Husband keeps his thoughts, words, and faith in line with what he is expecting, and then trust You to take care of it. In Jesus' name I pray, Amen.

• • •

May the words of my mouth and the meditation of my heart be pleasing to you, O Lord, my rock, and my redeemer.
Psalm 19:14

DAY 356

Dear God,

Fill the atmosphere with faith and victory instead of fear and defeat. I pray that My Husband receives according to your promises and that My Husband uses the gifts You have given him to be a blessing to our family, the community, and this world. May My Husband forever be the first and not the last, above, and not beneath. In Jesus' name I pray, Amen.

* * *

"Give, and you will receive. Your gift will return to you in full pressed down, shaken together to make room for more, running over, and poured into your lap. The amount you give will determine the amount you get back."
Luke 6:38

DAY 357

Dear God,

I pray that My Husband is a righteous man whose prayers are powerful and effective. Teach him to be a man devoted to prayer, watchful for your responses and thankful for your answers. In Jesus' name I pray, Amen.

• • •

I will study your commandments and reflect on your ways. I will delight in your decrees and not forget your word.
Psalm 119:15-16

TRUST

DAY 358

Dear God,

You wake us early to provide instructions and insights. I pray that My Husband looks forward to spending time with You at the start of each day, worshipping You and meditating on your Word.
In Jesus' name I pray, Amen.

• • •

I stay awake through the night,
thinking about your promise.
Psalm 119:48

DAY 359

Dear God,

We create reality by our prayers and our words. Help My Husband commit to honor You with his thinking, his words, and his prayers. I pray that My Husband receives all You have prepared for him—there will be no holdups, setbacks, or delays.
In Jesus' name I pray, Amen.

• • •

But when you pray, go away by yourself, shut the door behind you, and pray to your Father in private. Then your Father, who sees everything, will reward you.
Matthew 6:6

DAY 360

Dear God,

My Husband is moving toward your perfect plan. No matter what it looks like in the natural realm, I pray that he walks by faith and not by sight. May My Husband keep on believing until your will manifests in his life.
In Jesus' name I pray, Amen.

• • •

And it is impossible to please God without faith. Anyone who wants to come to him must believe that God exists and that he rewards those who sincerely seek him.
Hebrews 11:6

DAY 361

Dear God,

Remove any worry or anxiety from My Husband's shoulders. Remind him that You have great things stored up for him. Rather than feeling like he must carry the weight of the world on his shoulders, help My Husband to trust in your abundant provision. In Jesus' name I pray, Amen.

• • •

Give all your worries and cares to God, for he cares about you.
1 Peter 5:7

TRUST

DAY 362

Dear God,

When My Husband begins to feel the weight of the world on his shoulders, I pray that he seeks You, calls out to You, and depends on You. Deliver him from all his fears, worries, and anxieties and teach him to trust in You.
In Jesus' name I pray, Amen.

* * *

Then Jesus said, "Come to me, all of you who are weary and carry heavy burdens, and I will give you rest. Take my yoke upon you. Let me teach you, because I am humble and gentle at heart, and you will find rest for your souls. For my yoke is easy to bear, and the burden I give you is light."
Matthew 11:28-30

DAY 363

Dear God,

Your Word says that those who seek You will lack no good thing. Thank You for the promise. I pray that My Husband will not carry the burden of trying to meet all his needs on his own. Remind him to trust in your promised provision and care.
In Jesus' name I pray, Amen.

• • •

Even strong young lions sometimes go hungry, but those who trust in the Lord will lack no good thing.
Psalm 34:10

DAY 364

Dear God,

Your Word says that as You begin to work within us, for our growth we will face obstacles to overcome in prayer. Help My Husband to respond to challenging situations and show You just how large of an assignment he can be trusted with. My Husband is prepared for the mission; empower him to overcome each test. Cause him to grow in You so he will be fit. In Jesus' name I pray, Amen.

• • •

Dear brothers and sisters, when troubles of any kind come your way, consider it an opportunity for great joy. For you know that when your faith is tested, your endurance has a chance to grow. So, let it grow, for when your endurance is fully developed, you will be perfect and complete, needing nothing.
James 1:2-4

DAY 365

Dear God,

We know that the supernatural realm is where victories are won. So, I pray for victory over every 'Goliath' in My Husband's life—in our family, his finances, his work, his partnerships, his ministry, and his body. In Jesus' name I pray, Amen.

• • •

Do not be afraid, for I am with you.
Do not be discouraged, for I am
your God. I will strengthen you
and help you. I will hold you up
with my victorious right hand.
Isaiah 41:10

TRUST

www.ingramcontent.com/pod-product-compliance
Lightning Source LLC
Chambersburg PA
CBHW071949070526
44583CB00015B/1122